WE'VE BEEN MISLED:
Eating Healthy is Simple

ROBIN DOBBINS

Gotham Books

30 N Gould St.
Ste. 20820, Sheridan, WY 82801
https://gothambooksinc.com/

Phone: 1 (307) 464-7800

© 2024 *Robin Dobbins*. All rights reserved.

No part of this book may be reproduced, stored in a retrieval system, or transmitted by any means without the written permission of the author.

Published by Gotham Books (October 5, 2024)

ISBN: 979-8-3303-3844-3 (H)
ISBN: 979-8-3303-3842-9 (P)
ISBN: 979-8-3303-3843-6 (E)

Because of the dynamic nature of the Internet, any web addresses or links contained in this book may have changed since publication and may no longer be valid.

The views expressed in this work are solely those of the author and do not necessarily reflect the views of the publisher, and the publisher hereby disclaims any responsibility for them.

Table of Contents

Foreword iv
Acknowledgments xi
Introduction.. xiv
What is inflammation? 1
Monosodium Glutamate (MSG)... 9
High Fructose Corn Syrup... 17
Trans Fatty Acids (TFAs) 20
Sample Meal Plans Comparisons....................................... 26
The Worst Choices.. 30
The Great Equalizers 37
Blenderize Your Vegetables.. 43
Glycemic Load... 46
Anti-inflammatory Foods (Good Guys)................................ 48
Pro-Inflammatory Foods (Bad Guys)................................... 80
Poor Fast Food Choices... 137
Summary 142

Foreword

It's imperative for the readers of this book be made aware of the motivation and purpose for it becoming a publication, something I will share with you later in this Foreword. There are a thousand plus other books on the market, written more in depth by some of the most educated dieticians and nutritionists, all of whom are incredibly loaded with information on food combinations and their affects, nutrient breakdowns of thousands of foods, and seven-day meal plans and food recipes. One can easily say, my book was not written to gain market share or notoriety.

Sometime in late 1999, while lifting weights at 24 Hour Fitness in Pasadena, Texas (corner of Spencer Highway and Preston Road), a gentleman asked that I come to see him at his health food/supplement store on Pasadena Boulevard. Said he had a proposition for me to consider. Told me it would more than be worth my while. So, with much skepticism, I took time to visit his store and listen to the proposal.

He acknowledged my being a once locally known bodybuilder, but more importantly, liked the way I interfaced with people, helping them get the most out of their training. Then came the reason he asked me to see him. The man planned to open a huge gym to go along with his supplement store. He wanted me to manage the facility as a fifty-percent partner, plus a $100,000 salary. There was one condition; I had to enroll in Baylor Sports Medicine Institute's personal trainer and rehabilitative exercise specialist programs. I acquiesced willingly, enrolling in 2000 and finishing in 2002. It was without a doubt, the most difficult undertaking in my whole life. Fewer than 30% prevailed. The programs were scrapped shortly after I finished, due to the low success rate.

I am not going to bore you as to why the gym did not materialize, but it wasn't due to lack of finances. The man was made of money. That, however, left me remaining at

Lyondell Chemical for 35 years, working shift-work as a board operator. In the long run, God knew best. Gyms are not the best investments.

Here's where the story begins. I decided to become a part-time personal trainer for hire and ended up rehabbing people for knee replacements, back surgeries, rotator cuff surgeries, meniscus surgeries, shoulder and hip replacements, and an assortment of spinal problems, including sciatica (piriformis syndrome). The number of people wanting my services was daunting. Working a four on and four off schedule, allowed for this activity.

I worked out of the LaPorte, Texas Community Fitness and Senior Center for 20 years. It was the finest community health center I have ever been associated with. LaPorte itself is a rather unique city with a population of about 34,000. The fitness center was a great place for the older population to work out and socialize. More importantly, along with the senior center and its activities, the facility was about people having a place to go as an outlet from our chaotic, hectic world; a much needed refuge.

My clients, over the years, ranged from an eight year-old female figure skater to a 93 year-old woman with Alzheimer's. I ended up with a niche of 60 plus age clients, most of whom stayed with me for 15-20 years without a break. One woman told me, "You know more about your women clients than their gynecologists do." She was quite correct. I was someone to talk to on an intimate level about all subjects, and they were not embarrassed.

One day in 2014, while feeling so bogged down with questions on nutrition, I decided to publish some kind of food book to hand them, no charge. I had already logged a few hundred hours of seminars on the wide subject, read numerous books and hundreds of articles. Not to mention, the hard copy newsletters delivered to my mailbox and email newsletters. After reviewing the mountains of information, I made a decision. The mission was to produce something easy to understand and simple to execute. My two go-to sources were Ross Querry (PT, Ph.D.) and Ronald J. Grabowski (B.S., RD, DC). Both are renowned and live in the Houston area, making them accessible with their graciousness to help. Their seminars were loaded with helpful information that could be applied in the real world where most of us live.

After a few weeks of starting rough drafts, I remembered a food topic in one of my issues of the 'Blaylock Wellness Report'. It was a hard copy delivered to my mailbox. After searching through my bound collection, I found the September 2011 issue of the body's diseases being caused by dietary inflammation. Mainstream health had not yet focused on the subject. Dr. Russell Blaylock was a renowned neurosurgeon, health practitioner, author, and lecturer. He was the recipient of the Integrity in Science Award in 2004 and serves on editorial staffs of the Journal of the American Nutraceutical Association, Surgical Neurology International, the International Society for Fluoride Research, and the Journal of American Physicians.

It's here I decided to focus my food book content. It was more important to eat in such a way as to help avoid bodily inflammation. The strenuous research began, and I divided the book into anti-inflammatory foods, foods that fight inflammation, and pro-inflammatory foods, those of which cause inflammation. Each group contains the five main food groups; meat, starch, milk, fruit, and carbohydrates.

It just so happens, anti-inflammatory foods do contribute to weight loss, as experienced by many of my "victims" (clients). So, as it turns out, eating properly is easy after all. Few families have time for food measuring (recipes), preparing for their seven-day meal plan, and other schemes, such as worrying about food combining. Parents come home from work and confront their children's extracurricular activities, homework, baths, fixing supper, and putting children to bed. No time available to play chef.

Originally, the book was supposed to be a thin paperback to roll up and place in purses and back pockets. Somehow a hardback has appeared. You can email me at stirringbooksbyrobin@gmail.com, and you will receive answers to any questions you may have. The word "books" is plural, because I have two fresh novels for purchase on the website; one has a trailer.

Health & Fitness Background

In the summer of 1968, my wife, Janel, and I moved from our native state, Texas, to the San Francisco Bay Area so that I could play football and baseball for the University of California at Berkeley. Janel immediately procured a job at a big mortgage company, Mason McDuffie, right across the street from the University. Things were looking good until I made my first trip to the athletic offices.

I had to fight my way through rioting, tear gas, burning, gunfire, National Guard and police with shields, rock throwing and bodies on the ground. I saw rioters pummeling police officers and bloodying their faces with bricks and other objects. I made my way to what looked like a large cafeteria/student union building. Inside were giant posters everywhere saying: GOD IS DEAD!

After talking with the AD, coaches in both sports, and numerous players, I decided to leave. It was too late to move back to Texas, so I entered Diablo Valley College in Pleasant Hill, and moved on to California State University at Hayward, where I received my Political Science degree in June 1972.

Immediately after enrolling in Diablo Valley College, I found a place to lift weights. The name of the place was the Sun Valley Health Spa, located in the Sun Valley Shopping Mall. It was heavily carpeted with chrome plated weight machines, dumbbells, benches, Olympic Bars, and plates. It was a palace.

After classes, I would drive a short distance to reach the place. It didn't take a long time for a well-built instructor to approach me, urging I become a competitor. One day he gave me the street address of a gym in Oakland. Told me to see a guy named Jack, who was expecting me. I did not connect the dots. It was the world famous 'Father of Fitness,' Jack LaLanne. I did not find this out until he met me at the front desk. To say I was greatly intimidated would be a huge understatement.

He didn't shake my hand, but said, "So you're the guy Shea Patterson recommended I mentor. Well, son, you and I will be spending the next four weeks seeing if you have what it takes. It won't be easy and neither is success." He was the friendliest and most energetic guy I had ever met or ever will meet. Those four weeks were the most grueling four weeks of my life and my afterlife. Crossing the finish line on bloody nubs and vomit stained face, that most gracious and humble man, passed me off to Jack Dellinger for some more refining.

Mr. Dellinger was the 1956 'Mr. Universe'. He had blonde hair and a square jaw. He was what today I call a "No baloney "Toni". That man made me trade vomit for bloody eyes. I was bench pressing on one occasion and deadlifting on another, when blood literally squirted from one of my eyes. Squats were something else. One day he had me do heavy "cheats", where you lower yourself just about 4-6 inches and return to the upright position. At 700 lbs., I could neither breathe in nor exhale. I just knew my hemorrhoids were going to grow to the size of bowling balls.

It was at this point, I began to embrace workouts no mentally competent man would dare attempt. Suddenly, I was proud of being a Spartan, unfit for public service.

Mr. Dellinger then recommended me to the great promoter of bodybuilding, Joe Weider. So, off to Venice Beach and a place they called the 'Dungeon'. Joe was always looking for another horse for his unbelievable stable of thoroughbreds. At this time Arnold Schwarzenegger had just come on the scene.

After two weeks, I called Janel to tell her, professional bodybuilding was too consuming for my other desires in life, mainly her. I did love the camaraderie during the intense workouts.

Years later, Dave Draper (my favorite) and I exchanged emails regularly. I visited Larry Scott (the first 'Mr. Olympia') in Salt Lake City when searching for gym equipment. He was a consultant for a high dollar builder called Hogan. Both guys died within the past three years, Dave from extended years of heart problems, and Larry from Parkinson's.

Early in the fall of 1980, some bodybuilding contest judges approached me encouraging I think about hitting the contest trail, targeting Mr. America in 18 months. Endorsements were there, which would allow Janel to be a stay-at-home mom. However, it involved taking anabolic steroids. They were not illegal until 1986.

I acquiesced, after much consideration, but eight months later the side effects were horrible. After a heart-to-heart talk with a retired physician, I quit "cold turkey". I was taking Dianabol by mouth and Deca-Durabolin by injection.

For someone who has never partaken in such drugs, they cannot possibly imagine the dynamic power they offer, both physically and mentally. For women suffering from severe PMS, I truly can relate.

For those who are riding the rail between being vegan or a meat eater, let me leave you with this hard cold fact. No vegetable contains either the eight essential amino acids or the branch-chain amino acids. Amino acids are necessary for building muscle mass. It takes muscle mass to move the skeleton. As one ages, preserving and building muscle mass is imperative for continued mobility.

Whey protein shakes, eggs, and dairy will suffice in place of actual meat consumption. Red meat offers more size and strength due to the creatine content not found in the other meats. If you avoid red meat, supplement creatine. This nutrient has, among other things, benefits for the brain.

Gotta stop here, or this will become a book. Happy eating.

Acknowledgments

I want to thank Janel Dobbins for her amazing perseverance, diligence, and skill in word processing this book from my hand- written hen-scratch. Each chapter had to be redone numerous times due to my mistakes and re-editing. I know there were times she just wanted this project to mercifully end; so did I. In case you didn't catch her last name, this wonderful woman is my wife and best friend.

I can't thank enough the authors of the following books and newsletters for their unbelievable research and knowledge. They inspired this meager attempt to make things simple for my clients and people like them.

Books & Hard Copy Newsletters To My Home Mailbox

The Inflammation Free Diet Plan
 By Monica Reinagel
 Julius Torelli, M.D. (Consulting Editor)

The Blaylock Wellness Report
 (Hard copy to my home mailbox)
 By Dr. Russell Blaylock, Renowned Neurosurgeon
 Health Practitioner, Author, Lecturer

Ronald J. Grabowski, B.S., RD, DC
 Worldwide lecturer on nutritional health and founder of Innovative Nutritional Products.

 Attended two of his extraordinary seminars presented by Professional Fitness Instructor Training (PFIT). Sent three extremely overweight clients to him for dietary control and he worked wonders.

The Mind Health Report (Hard copy to my home mailbox)
  By Dr. Gary Small, Professor of Psychiatry & Aging
  Director of UCLA Longevity Center

Trans Fat: The Hidden Killer in Our Food
  By Judith Shaw, M.A.

Toxic Relief
  By Don Colbert, M.D.

What You Don't Know May Be Killing You
  By Don Colbert, M.D.

Advanced Sports Nutrition
  By Dan Bernardot, Ph.D., RD, FACSM

Power Eating
  By Susan M. Kleiner, Ph.D., RD
  With Maggie Greenwood-Robinson

Eating on the Run
  By Evelyn Tribole, MS, RD

The Maker's Diet
  By Jordan S. Rubin
  Foreword by Charles Stanley

The Carbohydrate Addict's Healthy Heart Program
  By Dr. Richard F. Heller
  Dr. Rachael F. Heller Dr. Frederic J. Vagnini

The Glucose Revolution
  By Helen O'Connor
  Jenner Brand-Miller, Ph.D. Stephen Colagiuri, M.D.
  Kay Foster-Powell, M.Nutr. & Diet
  Thomas M.S. Wolever, M.D. Ph.D.

Health Science Institute
  (Hard copy to my home mailbox)

E-Mail newsletters (countless articles):

Natural Health News & Self-Reliance About Health: Tip of the Day
Doctor's House Call – Al Sears, M.D.
Life Script
BioTrust Nutrition Life Enhancement
Dr. Whitaker newsletter

Introduction

There are 20,000 diet plans "out there" (i.e. Mediterranean, Paleo) and growing. Actually, several research groups put the number at 27,000. The Barnes & Noble bookstores have shelves upon shelves of books presenting these programs instructing us on eating correctly and combining foods properly. I have a cabinet filled with books on fitness and health; at least a dime's worth presenting diets and eating schemes alone. Many are designed to help one with the rather arduous task of keeping up with calories consumed and calories about to be consumed, while at the same time choosing foods that are truly nutritious. After all, it's highly possible to devour a bunch of "nutrition-empty" calories as your health eventually wanes. From there, the onslaught of publications covers carb counting, the glycemic index guide, diet cycling, fasting, juicing, "veganing," high- protein low-carb, and sundry of other topics. Ultimately, the emphasis is on changing the image of one's body composition from unfavorable to favorable through a sound eating and fitness regimen.

Wrong emphasis! These considerations will not help you avoid the silent but gradual erosion toward Alzheimer's, Parkinson's, heart disease, arthritis and an assortment of other crippling diseases that surface after age 50; ruining your "Golden Years." INFLAMMATION at the cellular level of both body and brain is the real felon, but yet is the least recognized or written about by mainstream health and fitness movers and shakers. It is without argument, amongst neurosurgeons and researchers alike, caused by the food we eat. If you eat to avoid inflammation, you'll not only avoid being disabled later in life, but your body composition will fall into place as well.

Each and every work mentioned above results from hours upon hours of research culminating in incredibly valuable scholarship to support the claims. These books are very meticulously thought out. Most of the authors have sincere intentions toward helping promote good health as well as procuring some financial reward. And rightfully so, because the provision of this much needed knowledge will not be researched out by the readers; they have nowhere near time nor the gumption, mostly the gumption. Yet, the urgency for this valuable information and direction is unquestionable, regardless if the "readers-in-need" realize the immediate necessity for adopting a reasonably healthy design for eating. Eventually, we are talking about a quality life, because "Father Time" does indeed close the gap between youth and old age. The older you become, the more imperative your food choices measure up to quality nutrients, while avoiding being of the inflammatory nature.

Unfortunately, youth is wasted on the young, who feel bullet-proof and have no fear of eating irresponsibly. By the time wisdom, knowledge, and reason catch up to them, obesity or old age (maybe both) has arrived with all its ailments. The reality is: for some it's too late; their diseases, ailments, or obesity cannot be reversed. That evolution is fatal. This book is not for the under 45 years of age group; those will only question the validity of this dissertation since they have no visible ailments. These are hardcore skeptics with no access to real knowledge.

If you read the "Foreword," you know I was a personal fitness trainer and rehabilitative exercise specialist. Working "for hire" at a community fitness center combined with a senior citizen recreation- activity facility for 20 years has opened my eyes beyond what I previously believed. I have had the misfortune of knowing healthy men and women (on the surface) at ages 45-50 and watching them hit the bottom at 60-65. They have gone from working out in the fitness center to playing dominos in the senior center, using a walker or scooter to get there. Six of my beloved clients have died of disease during this time. All the schemes to change your body from obese to skinny cannot prevent the slide. There are as many crippled lean people as there are disabled overweight people. Therefore, let me please emphasize, body composition evolving from unfavorable to favorable is no indication of a healthy body and brain. Dr. Russell Blaylock (renowned Neurosurgeon) will explain inflammation and its unseen devastation in the following chapter. Hopefully it will alarm you.

It's easy to accept weightlifting as 30% of the process for good health and a judicious diet as 70%. Almost everyone can agree with that, but they cannot find the time to work out, and are too stressed out to eat properly. We live in a technological world that is running at breakneck speed with increasing demands on our body and mind. Our answer to the imposing question about finding time to work out and eat nutritiously is: 'As soon as I find time,' or 'If I can just get a few of these things done.' It never happens – there is no perfect time to begin the groundwork to prevent the inevitable mudslide that washes your body and mind to oblivion.

Like the book's narration, this introduction is short and to-the-point. The goal here amounts to simplifying intelligent food choices in an effort to live a healthy life and stave off disease. With **INFLAMMATION** now the inarguable "father of all disease," it will be necessary to examine the scientific explanations. Alarmingly, an overwhelming number of nutritious whole foods are the culprit and architect of this "deadly" condition. In addition, the three most dangerous processed food additives, **trans fatty acids (TFAs), high fructose corn syrup (HFCS), and MSG (monosodium glutamate)** also spearhead the expeditious development of inflammation. These (known as excitotoxins) too will be discussed, including the science, foods they occupy, and "secret" names manufacturers use on labels.

Just how dangerous is inflammation? Unanimous hard scientific data unequivocally blames this guy for:

- Osteoarthritis
- Rheumatoid arthritis
- Eczema or psoriasis
- Asthma
- Allergies
- Heart disease
- High blood pressure
- High cholesterol
- Alzheimer's disease
- Parkinson's disease
- Diabetes
- Cancer
- Joint pain or stiffness

As a sidelight, for those interested in blood sugar effects of the various carbohydrates, a short section will explain the term "glycemic load," which has replaced the outdated "glycemic index." This is very important for those who wisely fear diabetes.

There are neither daily meal plans nor recipes offered, but the foods listed do come with portion sizes. There is no need for counting calories. Eating was not meant to be a complex task, where preparation requires a well-equipped laboratory with food weight scales and calculators. The planning necessary to shop for grub should not be a monumental challenge. The victuals outlined in this work are divided into two groups; anti-inflammatory promoting and inflammatory causing (pro-inflammatory). Every food will have what researchers refer to as an IF Rating (Inflammatory Rating) to go along with a glycemic load indication (GL). The inflammatory food will be designated with a minus sign in front of its number. The anti-inflammatory food will be designated by a positive number; no plus sign.

To graze from the anti-inflammatory group, ensures avoiding inflammation as well as escaping HFCS, TFAs, MSG, counting calories, worrying about carbohydrates, and concerning one's self with portion sizes. However, there are popular nutritious foods that are inflammatory, and the task of the reader is to simply juggle the food choices in such a way as to stay on the positive side - anti-inflammatory. In other words, at the end of the day, week, or month, your IF Rating should average out on the plus side. For example, if on a given day you consume two foods that together total -30 and follow with two foods whose rating together adds up to a 50, then your total for the day was a successful 20. How hard could that be? A section on sample meals with similar food choices is presented; one pro-inflammatory and the other anti-inflammatory by changing one item. Another small section presents the worst choices, and still one more offers the **Great Equalizers**; food items so high on the anti-inflammatory scale, they can more than offset a would-be pro-inflammation meal. And by the way, for those concerned about body image, you too will be happy. Those not concerned with body image will just have to accept not being obese.

The real problem amongst the pro-inflammatory lists lies within the processed foods. Here is where the deadliest of the silent assassins reside, lurking in the shadows.

Hope you find the content of this text informative and easy to read and understand.

Stay positive, my friend.

Honesty is the first chapter in the book of Wisdom
- Thomas Jefferson

BAYLOR SPORTS MEDICINE INSTITUTE

Recognizes

Robin Dobbins

For successfully demonstrating nationally accepted requirements through a comprehensive examination of theoretical knowledge and practical applications for personal training of the general, apparently healthy population, the above named is hereby recognized as a

Certified Personal Fitness Trainer
BSMI-CPFT

Valid Through
07/31/2002

BAYLOR SPORTS MEDICINE INSTITUTE

BAYLOR SPORTS MEDICINE INSTITUTE

Recognizes

Robin Dobbins

For successfully demonstrating nationally accepted requirements through a comprehensive examination of theoretical knowledge and practical applications of advanced understanding and enhanced skills in rehabilitative exercise continuums for the specialized needs of a general, apparently healthy population having experienced an acute or chronic injury, the above named is hereby recognized as a

Rehabilitative Exercise Specialist-Certified
BSMI-RES-C

Valid Through
10/31/03

BAYLOR SPORTS MEDICINE INSTITUTE

What is inflammation?

Inflammation is the first response of your immune system to infection or irritation (also injury). All of us are familiar with the classic signs of this condition (swelling, redness and pain). Blood and fluid rush to the injured site transporting healing nutrients.

This defense mechanism comes to the rescue when your body's surveillance system detects a foreign body, such as bacterium or virus (infection), invading its territory. Redness and swelling around an infected region is caused by millions of white blood cells speeding toward a site with the purpose of overpowering an intruder. The presence of fever indicates a sort of whole-body inflammation predicated to overcoming the menace. By raising the temperature of the body significantly, the bug will succumb to heatstroke.

Through a sprained ankle (irritation and injury), you have probably witnessed another impressive display of the body's response. An ankle can swell to the size of a melon within minutes, functioning to act as a splint for protective immobilization. As any orthopedist will tell you, doctors don't heal sprained ankles; they just supervise while nature and time do their jobs. Pain is nothing more than a signal to stop what you're doing, thereby avoiding further damage.

These examples of inflammation have a useful purpose, and the swelling gradually subsides and vanishes. No harm; job done.

Undesirable Inflammation Not in Your Control

Obviously, you don't want to diminish the body's protective and healing powers. But it's a must to eliminate excessive, chronic, and inappropriate inflammation. All kinds of arthritis, for example, are characterized by painful swelling and stiffness in joints. Allergies are another sort of non-productive inflammatory responses in which the immune system tries to attack otherwise harmless substances like pollen or animal dander. These kinds of inflammation serve no useful purpose and can make your life miserable. Over time, excessive inflammation (whatever the cause) increases your risk of several life- threatening diseases, **but at least you are aware of such attacks from inflammation.**

Undesirable Inflammation In Your Control (Food Consumption)

Recent research has shown eating the wrong foods does cause chronic inflammation within our bodies (at the cellular level). This chronic inflammation is not so obvious. It is the dreaded, more dangerous form – a silent, invisible assassin that destroys every facet of your body (yes, especially the brain) for years without revealing the slightest symptom. Eventually, though, the damage will expose itself in the form of heart disease, Alzheimer's disease, or cancer, to name a few.

Our cells produce a variety of pro and anti-inflammatory chemicals called prostaglandins, using nutrients from the food we eat as the raw material. These prostaglandins are released into our tissues, responding to the immune system's signals, promoting inflammation where there is danger and quelling inflammation, when the danger has passed.

In the April 2010 issue of the **Blaylock Wellness Report**, the prominent neurosurgeon Dr. Russell Blaylock writes:

"There is growing evidence that chronic, smoldering inflammation is a major cause of frailty in the elderly. Remember – where there is inflammation there is massive generation of free radicals and lipid peroxidation products (caustic fats) that are flooding the body – every organ and tissue. They always go together.

These nasty particles and caustic fats not only destroy parts of cells, they also destroy the glue that holds us together – that is, our ligaments, bones, joints, and connective tissue of our skin (causing wrinkles).

Over time, our tissues and organs become so weakened that we begin to break apart like wet sand on a beach. This process doesn't happen overnight; it happens over decades."

This is a rather ugly, gruesome depiction of the reality surrounding this "skipped over" subject matter involving the foods we eat. Dr. Blaylock will be heard from again in this book.

A key concept in this oversimplified portrayal is our bodies produce prostaglandins by using compounds from the foods we eat. Specifically, it is the fatty acids in our foods which our bodies use to make prostaglandins. Certain types of fatty acids (primarily those from the Omega 6 family) are converted into pro-inflammatory prostaglandins, while other types (primarily from the Omega 3 family) are used to make anti-inflammatory prostaglandins. Also, but not minimally, inflammation does develop through diets dominated by processed/packaged foods filled with the three most lethal food additives mentioned in the Introduction: monosodium glutamate, high fructose corn syrup, and trans fatty acids. Mercifully, nature has provided the antidote; foods that are just as effective at reversing inflammation.

Conditions Characterized by Excessive Inflammation Regardless of the Cause

- Heart Disease
- Alzheimer's disease
- Cancer
- Obesity
- Diabetes
- Autoimmune Diseases
- Asthma
- Allergies
- Arthritis
- Prostate Disease

The "IF" (Inflammatory) System to the Rescue

The "IF" Rating system was developed in an effort to make it easier for a non-specialist to understand the inflammatory or anti- inflammatory effects facilitated by a wide variety of foods. Each is given an "IF" rating number, representing the net inflammatory or anti-inflammatory impact of that food.

The "good guys" are foods represented by a positive number, and the "bad guys" have a negative designation. IF ratings between 1 and 100 possess mildly anti-inflammatory properties. Numbers between 101 and 500 are moderately anti-inflammatory, and those over 500 are strongly anti-inflammatory. On the other end of the scale, numbers ranging between -1 and -100 are mildly inflammatory. Foods ranging between -101 and -500 prove to be moderately inflammatory, and ones showing -500 and above are considered strongly inflammatory. It makes sense these two rosters are made available in this book and should be the backbone to simplify your making good decisions concerning eating healthy foods, while avoiding horrific disease causing inflammatory ones. Poor decisions will catch up to you; make no mistake. Should you have doubts or be a mighty skeptic, be more observant when venturing out to the grocery store or settling in at your favorite restaurant. Go to a fitness center and take inventory of whose participating in water aerobics. Crippling obesity dominates the scene, but amazingly, those few who look fit and trim may be just as disabled. So feast your eyes upon those aforementioned, because they are mirroring what you will look like someday should inflammation causing foods heavily dot your meals and snacks. Roll the dice with boisterous flare, but you will be the loser.

How the IF Rating is Calculated

The IF Rating integrates more than twenty (20) different pro- inflammatory and anti-inflammatory factors. The amounts of individual nutrients are considered, as well as the ratios between various nutrients. The formula also incorporates the glycemic load, which describes the impact a food has on blood sugar; whether it causes blood sugar to rise sharply or slowly. It also takes into consideration processed/packaged foods (especially) containing a relatively new concept: "**excitotoxins;**" monosodium glutamate, high fructose corn syrup, and trans fats being the main culprits.

Where does all of this information come from? The U.S. Department of Agriculture. The USDA has conducted extensive nutritional analyses on thousands of raw, processed, and commercially prepared foods. These measurements make up the National Nutritional Database for Standard Reference and are used as the basis of virtually all nutritional databases in our country. The most recent update for the database (SR17) was published in

2004 and provides considerable details used in calculations of those IF Ratings.

Determining Your Level of Systemic Inflammation

C-reactive protein (CRP) is a compound in the blood signaling the presence of nonspecific systemic inflammation. Elevated levels of CRP are a serious warning inflammation is gathering significantly somewhere in the body. Fortunately, there are medical tests that can measure the presence of inflammation long before a serious disease has developed. This can be done with a rather affordable, reliable blood test, which has become the most widely used measure of systemic inflammation.

Fibrinogen, a compound that indicates the propensity of blood to form clots, is sometimes used as a secondary indication inflammation is present, especially in heart patients. As with CRP, higher levels of fibrinogen suggest increased inflammation. And most recently, researchers have discovered elevated white blood cell counts indicate an increased risk of inflammation related disease, particularly in women. Different test combinations can provide a physician with a nuanced picture of the patient's inflammatory processes. In general, however, a simple CRP test is entirely sufficient to screen for and track the presence of systemic inflammation. Many physicians will include a CRP test in your annual blood workup if you ask. In fact, it is recommended those over forty (40) have this done, especially if you have a family history of the diseases referred to in these narrations.

Understanding Your Test Results

The CRP test is not a test for any particular disease or condition. It will not state whether you have heart disease, cancer, or Alzheimer's disease. This test will simply indicate whether you have an excessive level of systemic inflammation.

CRP is usually measured in milligrams per liter (mg/L). Ideally you want your CRP levels to be in the "no risk" to "slightly risky" range (.55-1.14) for men and "no risk" (<1.5) for women. As you can see, in the table provided, even slight elevations of CRP have been tied to an increased risk of heart attack, stroke, and other diseases.

Important Note: Any infection or injury will cause a temporary rise in your CRP levels as the body's immune system responds to the crisis. If you experience an acute infection or injury, wait two weeks before scheduling a CRP test to ensure an accurate result.

CRP Levels and Disease Risks

Men

CRP	Risk of Future Heart Attack
0.55 mg/L or less	No increased risk; ideal
0.56-1.14 mg/L	Slightly more likely
1.15-2.10 mg/L	2 ½ times as likely
2.11 mg/L and higher	3 times as likely

Women

CRP	Risk of Future Heart Attack or Stroke
Less than 1.50 mg/L	No increased risk; Ideal
1.50-3.79 mg/L	2 ½ times as likely
3.80-7.30 mg/L	3 ½ times as likely
7.31 mg/L and higher	5 ½ times as likely

Monosodium Glutamate (MSG)

Monosodium glutamate is a naturally occurring salt form of glutamate, which makes it highly absorbable. But it is the glutamate in MSG that causes toxicity. All forms of glutamate, natural or artificial, are equally harmful if glutamate (glutamic acid) is isolated.

The difference is natural glutamate found in whole foods rarely appears alone. It is always combined with other substances to create a complex protein. For natural glutamate to be released, it must experience digestion. This releases the glutamate slowly, allowing the body time to deal with it safely.

Cooking high-glutamate foods, such as red meats, tomatoes, and mushrooms, allows the glutamate to be released and even concentrated - as in meat juices (broth and stocks) and vegetable extracts (hydrolyzed proteins and soy protein isolates and extracts). These forms of glutamate can be just as toxic as MSG.

In the words of Dr. Russell Blaylock, a nationally recognized, board-certified neurosurgeon, health practitioner, author, and lecturer; "When I first wrote my book, 'Excitotoxins: The Taste That Kills,' scientists were just beginning to learn how glutamate damaged the nervous system and the brain. Since then, we have learned an enormous amount about the function of glutamate in the brain and how it can cause damage - sometimes permanent when present in excess amounts."

In 1969, neuroscientist Dr. John Olney of the Washington University School of Medicine first discovered the manner in which excess glutamate destroys brains cells. He called this process **excitotoxicity**. Dr. Olney called the process by this name because when he added small amounts of monosodium glutamate to brain cells in a culture, the cells began to shrivel up and die after about an hour. He noted that just before this happened, the neurons were firing very rapidly, suggesting they were burning up themselves. Hence the name combining the root words excito (excite) and toxicity (poison).

Glutamate receptors (glutamate) are now being shown to play a major role in a growing list of neurological and psychiatric disorders, including:

- Alzheimer's
- Parkinson's
- ALS, Huntington's
- Depression
- Anxiety
- Schizophrenia
- Obsessive - Compulsive Disorder
- Autism
- ADHD
- Chronic Pain
- Addiction
- Strokes
- Brain Injury

There is also a host of other health issues and dangers prevalent with MSG. This flavor enhancer is linked to:

- Fibromyalgia
- Obesity
- Fatty liver
- High insulin and blood sugar
- High cholesterol

- Liver toxicity
- Metabolic syndrome
- High blood pressure
- Disturbance to the gut-brain connection
- Neurological and brain damage

Hidden Names for MSG and Free Glutamic Acid

- Glutamic Acid
- Glutamate
- Monosodium Glutamate
- Monopotassium Glutamate
- Calcium Glutamate
- Monoammonium Glutamate
- Magnesium Glutamate
- Natrium Glutamate
- Yeast Extract
- Anything hydrolyzed
- Any hydrolyzed protein
- Calcium Caseinate
- Sodium Caseinate
- Yeast Food
- Yeast Nutrient
- Autolyzed Yeast
- Gelatin
- Textured Protein

- Soy Protein
- Soy Protein Concentrate
- Soy Protein Isolate
- Whey Protein
- Whey Protein Concentrate
- Whey Protein Isolate
- Anything protein
- Vetsin
- Ajinomoto

Names of Ingredients That Often Contain Manufactured Free Glutamic Acid

- Carrageenan
- Bouillon and broth
- Stock
- Any flavors or flavoring
- Maltodextrin
- Citric acid, Citrate
- Anything ultra-pasteurized
- Barley malt
- Pectin
- Protease
- Anything enzyme modified
- Anything containing enzymes
- Malt extract
- Soy sauce

- Soy sauce extract
- Anything protein fortified
- Anything fermented
- Seasonings

A number of natural substances found in plant based diets have been shown to be very **protective** against excitotoxicity. These include:

- Magnesium
- Selenium
- Vitamin B6
- Mixed tocopherols and tocotrienols
- B vitamins
- Methylcobalamin
- Folate
- Flavanoids
- Silymarin
- Baicalein
- Grape seed extract
- DHA
- Vitamin D3
- Hawthorn extract

The Science

Glutamate has been discovered to be the most abundant transmitter in the brain, accounting for more than 90% of the communication in the brain's cortex and more than 50% of all the grey matter's communication. Glutamate transmissions exceed those of all the other transmitters, such as acetylcholine, serotonin, dopamine, and norepinephrine combined. We're talking here about the glutamate inside the cell walls.

In the words of Dr. Blaylock, "Glutamate damages the brain cells only it if is outside the cell where the receptors are located. This glutamate comes from our food, especially the manufactured MSG. God equipped our brains with a number of protective mechanisms that keep glutamate mostly within brain cells. The ratio of inside to outside the brain cell is 1,000 to 1."

A number of other mechanisms also help protect the brain, most of which require a lot of energy. Brain disorders such as stroke, trauma, neurodegenerative diseases (Alzheimer's, Parkinson's), and heavy metal poisoning result in a loss of brain energy. People with these disorders risk damage to the brain from even small exposures to dietary excitotoxins.

As we age, our brain energy decreases, and protective systems begin to falter. The brain then becomes progressively more inflamed. Together, these factors make us extra sensitive to dietary excitotoxins, and our brains begin to leak glutamate from storage sites, primarily the glia, which are the brain's immune cells. This is why the incidence of Alzheimer's goes from 3%, at age 65, to 50% at age 80.

Exposure to high levels of glutamic acid in the diet may also explain the explosion of obesity among the young and even among older people. MSG additives via processed foods were introduced to the public on a grand scale in 1948. Now they are out of control, as virtually every major food manufacturer uses some other form of the excitotoxic additive, especially trans fats and high fructose corn syrup. When excitotoxic food additives are ingested, they take a journey from the gastrointestinal tract to the liver via the portal vein. This makes the liver very vulnerable to damage, because it is exposed to the highest concentration of glutamate. Studies have shown that dietary MSG significantly raises inflammation, and causes a massive production of free radicals and lipid peroxidation in the liver that can persist for a very long time. This increases the damage from other toxins.

Glutamate is also a cancer fertilizer and can alter the function of every cell in the body. Recent studies have shown glutamate is found in every tissue and organ in the body, including:

- Skin and bones
- GI tract
- Pancreas
- Liver
- Kidney
- Reproductive organs (testes and ovaries)
- Prostate
- Immune cells

When folks are sensitive to MSG, they are actually reacting to **free** glutamic acid in the blood. Remember, MSG is made when the **free** glutamic acid binds with a sodium molecule. Whenever protein is broken down in the body, glutamic acid is **freed** from a protein in which it naturally occurs. Consequently, you have the potential of free glutamic acid building up in the blood and a possible toxic MSG reaction.

While this happens naturally, when ingesting protein-rich whole foods like grains, meats, dairy, and even vegetables, the glutamic acid is released in concert with many other amino acids, rather than in high concentrations on its own. As a result, unadulterated whole-food-based proteins do not cause a toxic MSG reaction in the body.

On the other hand, many processed foods, including organic health foods, contain processed proteins that harbor free glutamic acids (toxins).

Remember, glutamic acid found in unadulterated "whole food" protein does not cause adverse reactions. To cause adverse reactions, the glutamic acid must have been processed/manufactured or come from protein that has been fermented.

The Beginning

MSG, or monosodium glutamate, got its reputation as a flavor enhancer extracted from seaweeds in China. The year 1908 saw the process perfected in Japan by Professor Kikunae Ikeda and became commercially available. Concentrated free glutamic acid or MSG act as nerve stimulants and will change how the taste buds embrace the food. A yucky or even a really foul flavored food will taste fantastic when high levels of glutamic acid are introduced.

In the 1960's, the phrase "Chinese Restaurant Syndrome" was coined by the New England Journal of Medicine. Twenty minutes after eating Chinese food, some people sensitive to MSG would experience tingling, numbness, brain fog, chest pressure, and pain.

By the 1970's, researchers found that pharmaceutical MSG would kill brain cells in a laboratory. Shortly thereafter, they realized commercially available MSG had the same effect.

Do you need any more convincing to by-pass the center aisles when touring the grocery store? Jack LaLane, one of the pioneers of health and fitness, once said, "If it's packaged, I don't eat it."

High Fructose Corn Syrup

The corn industry is desperately attempting to convince the public (as well as the FDA) high fructose corn syrup (HFCS) is a "natural" product and no more harmful for human consumption than cane sugar. "Corn people" argue their product is not the culprit it is made out to be. It has been acknowledged by all contending parties too much of either is bad. However, Dr. Bruce Ames, a renowned professor of Biochemistry and Molecular Biology Emeritus at the University of California, Berkley, and a senior scientist at Children's Hospital Oakland Research Institute has shared shocking new evidence from his research center how HFCS can trigger body-wide inflammation and obesity.

It is necessary to understand some basic biochemistry. Regular cane sugar (sucrose) is made of two-sugar molecules bound tightly together - glucose and fructose in equal amounts. The enzymes in your digestive tract must break down the sucrose into glucose and fructose, which are then absorbed into the body.

HFCS also consists of glucose and fructose. However, it is not in a 50/50 ratio, but a 55/45 fructose to glucose ratio in an **unbound form**. Fructose is sweeter than glucose. Since there is **no chemical bond** between them, digestion is not required, allowing both to more rapidly be absorbed into your blood stream. Fructose goes straight to the liver and triggers lipogenesis, the production of fats (triglycerides) and cholesterol. **This is why high fructose corn syrup is the major cause of liver damage in this country**. "Fatty Liver" affects over 70 million people. The rapidly absorbed glucose triggers big spikes in insulin - our body's major fat storage hormone. Both of these features of HFCS lead to increased metabolic disturbances that drive increase appetites, weight gain, diabetes, heart disease, cancer, accelerated aging, dementia, and more.

Also, high doses of free fructose (from HFCS) have been proven to literally punch holes in the intestinal lining, allowing **nasty** by- products of toxic gut bacteria and partially digested food proteins to enter your blood stream and ignite the inflammation that we know is at the root of all disease. **Naturally occurring fructose in fruit is part of a complex of nutrients and fiber that does not exhibit the same biological effects as the free high fructose doses found in "corn sugar."**

Production

Corn syrups, including HFCS, are made from corn starch. Commercial production of corn syrup began in 1864. During the late 1950's, scientists at Clinton Corn Processing Company in Iowa tried to transform glucose from corn starch into fructose, but the process was not scalable. In 1965 Yoshiyuki Tasasaki at the Japanese National Institute of Advanced Industrial Science and Technology (AIST) developed a heat-stable xylose isomerase enzyme from yeast, and three years later AIST partnered with the Clinton Company to successfully commercialize the process.

In the contemporary process, corn (maize) is milled to produce corn starch, and an "acid-enzyme" process is used causing the corn starch solution to become acidified to begin breaking up the existing carbohydrates. The corn starch is further metabolized to convert the resulting sugars into fructose. The first enzyme added is alpha- amylase which breaks the long chains down into shorter sugar chains - oligosaccharides. Glucoamylase is mixed in and converts them into glucose. The resulting solution is filtered to remove protein, using activated carbon, and then demineralized, using ion-exchange resins. The purified solution is then run over immobilized xylose isomerase, which turns the sugars to 50-52% glucose with some unconverted oligosaccharides, and 42% fructose (HFCS 42), and again demineralized and again purified using activated carbon. Some is processed into HFCS 90 by liquid chromatolography, then mixed with HFCS 42 to form HFCS 55. The enzymes used in the process are made by microbial fermentation.

If one fully follows this process, he or she is far ahead of my understanding. For myself, this was an exercise in futility; simply one to validate this short essay on a food researchers agree is highly toxic (especially with mercury).

Historical Background

Prior to the development of the worldwide sugar industry, dietary fructose was limited to only a few items. Milk, meats, and most vegetables, the staples of many early diets, have no fructose, and only 5-10% fructose by weight is found in fruits such as grapes, apples, blueberries. From 1970 to 2000 there was a 25% increase in added sugars in the U.S. After being classified as "generally recognized as safe," (GRAS) by the U.S. Food & Drug Administration in1976, HFCS began to replace sucrose (cane sugar) as the main sweetener in soft drinks in the U.S. by 1984. At the same time, obesity escalated.

HFCS is used worldwide as a sweetener due to being easier to handle than granulated sugar and less expensive due to the price of the raw material, corn, being subsidized by the government.

Trans Fatty Acids (TFAs)

According to a distressing report (July 2002) by the Institute of Medicine at the National Academy of Sciences, our government's adviser to health policy, Americans are ingesting foods with an ingredient which has zero acceptable levels of consumption - trans fatty acids (TFAs). This declaration resulted in the FDA handing down labeling requirements forcing manufacturers of processed foods to reveal the presence of this venomous additive by 2006.

Trans fatty acids are manufactured through a process called **hydrogenation**. Soy beans, safflower seeds, grapeseed (Canola), cottonseeds, corn, and sunflower seeds are crushed, producing pure vegetable oils. At this point, these oils are good for you as fatty acids. Now begins the poisonous process, honing the oils with chemical solvents to deodorize and bleach. A metal catalyst (ordinarily nickel) is added to speed up the chemical reaction of this solution. From there, the brew is subjected to extremely high pressure and heat, coupled with injection of hydrogen gas. Presto, you have a molecular reaction that produces a solid product at room temperature; no longer an oil at all, but a thick plastic.

These manufactured unnatural fats absolutely cause dysfunction - a Chinese Fire Drill at the cellular level in your body. The consequences of consistent consumption of TFAs are accumulatively catastrophic.

Cells in our bodies are distinguished by membranes, which are thin semi-permeable coverings enclosing a cell's contents. A membrane's function is to preserve the integrity of the cell by allowing certain substances to enter and chasing away others. These rascals are composed of oils, some protein, and various carbohydrates. The oils are continually renewed and replaced. Therefore, the human body's functions depend upon the oils we consume on a daily basis.

Cells must be flexible and respond instantly to hormones, inflammation, and other changes. The **flexibility** depends upon the kinds of oils allowed to enter the body. This flexibility enhances the presentation of the proper targets for which chemical messengers coordinate paramount bodily functions.

When **partially hydrogenated oils** (TFAs) stumble into our food intake, they too enter the cell membrane. The plastic TFAs also take up cell space preventing good fats from entering. Consequently, crucial membrane flexibility is replaced by stiffness, causing loss of ability to signal and respond effectively to life's requirements. Eventually, the human body will begin to break down. Inflammation of the cells begins to spread, causing innumerable metabolic nightmares.

What are these nightmares? How about embracing insulin resistance (Type II Diabetes), obesity, heart disease, autoimmune disease, cancer, asthma, bone degeneration, reproductive problems, cholesterol problems (lowering the "good" and increasing the "bad), and depression? Sound good? If so, keep eating the following:

All Packaged or Processed Foods Examples:

Breakfast Cereals	Quaker Oats Chewy Granola Bars
Saltine Crackers	Special K's entire line of health/weight loss food
Girl Scout Cookies	Pop Corn (Microwavable)
Animal Crackers	Fig Newtons (except fat-free version)
Ritz Crackers	Fortune Cookies
Frozen Pies, Pot Pies,	

Pie Crust	Frozen Pizza, Tacos
Many hamburger and hot dog buns	Cheesecake, Cornbread, Brownies
Any restaurant food cooked	

The good news is TFAs will be eliminated from your cells when you no longer eat foods comprising such. Given the opportunity, healthy fatty acids will eventually replace those horrible TFAs and more efficient cell function will be reinstated. The bad news is structural damage already done cannot be reversed.

It is true that much information in the field of health changes so often, one may hope someday there is some good in TFAs; that they're really not as bad as first thought. Unfortunately, the possibility here does not exist - ever. The substance is plastic.

It must also be noted that the FDA food label ruling on TFAs left the food manufacturers a slight "loop hole;" as long as the food has less than .50 grams of trans fat per serving, the label is allowed to read "0". That means .49 is legal per serving. This adds up quickly considering few people actually consume just one serving of any food.

Why do restaurants, especially fast food establishments, prefer to cook with trans-fat? They're cheap, can be used and continually reused, besides making fried foods crispier. The cost effective list is simply infinite.

Historical Background

The great Industrial Revolution of the late nineteenth century caused an enormous migration of rural people around the world to the urban manufacturing centers. This swell created unpredictable circumstances, especially for those seeking their fortune while leaving "the farm." Severe food shortages, housing scarcity, poor sanitation and health dominated the landscape along with crime.

New York City was a crowded slum rampant with disease, and the poor, uneducated, and hungry were poised for terrifying municipal unrest and gang wars. Paris saw people living on the verge of starvation. One slum outside Paris was referred to as the Siberia of Paris. Artisans and assembly line workers were frequently in distress with twelve hour days of hard labor, poor living conditions, and poor diet. Similar conditions existed in England and the rest of Europe.

Food shortages and the lack of animal fat for cooking were the monumental concerns. The French government led the way with huge sums of money toward grants for urging its scientists to solve the problems of food spoilage and the lack of fat with which to cook or bake. Food substitutes and preservation were the priorities.

One food the working class could not afford was animal fat - beef, butter, poultry fat, and lard from pigs. This scarcity meant the loss of an essential cooking and baking ingredient.

Napoleon III offered huge financial gifts to French scientists, encouraging the climate of investigation. A French chemist named Hippolyte Mege-Marries invented a product made completely from animal parts. Using an acid called margaric as part of the process, he named the miracle product margarine.

However, this margarine did not resemble butter nor lard which it was designed to replace. Unattractive and brownish in color, it was prone to becoming rancid. It also had the unfortunate fragrance of rendered meat parts. Though somewhat more affordable, it was still too expensive to produce. A new focus became crucial - how to replace this with something that would not spoil and yet less expensive to render.

In 1897, two French chemists, Jean Sabatier and Jean-Baptiste Sendrens, discovered there was more hydrogen in solid animal fats than vegetable oils. They wondered what would happen if hydrogen was added to vegetable oil. Could it make margarine?

Wilhelm Norman, a German scientist, heard about Sabatier's theory (an article) in 1901. He was able to transform liquid oleic acid (later known as oleo margarine) into solid stearic acid by the use of hydrogen and dispersed nickel. This was the precursor of saturated fat hardening. On February 27, 1901, he finalized the process and on August 14, 1902, secured a patent. From 1901 to 1909 he was head of the laboratory at Leprince & Siveke, where he conducted investigations of the properties of fats and oils.

TFAs were a miracle solution for food preservation and inexpensive cooking and baking oils for the poor. These oils needed no refrigeration, and foods processed with them could last years on the shelf. Long shelf life solved the problem of food shortages.

The Truth About TFAs; Why It Took So Long

In 1913, Proctor & Gamble, makers of Ivory soap, began to market Crisco. It was the first edible food product other than margarine manufactured with hydrogenated oils. It leaped in popularity during WWI and WWII due to animal fat and meat rationing. By the 1950s, the American Heart Association announced the United States was in the midst of a coronary heart disease epidemic. Once the cause of such was discovered, Crisco and other hydrogenated cooking oils were a Godsend.

When in 1956, President Eisenhower initiated the interstate highway system legislation, packaged foods could be transported across the nation and overseas without fear of spoilage.

But a biochemist named Mary Enig and a few concerned physicians in the late 1970s began to question whether there were adverse effects from manufactured trans fatty acids. Was the human body liking them?

Of course not, but the cover-up lasted over 20 years due to one and only one major reason: money. No one was falling down in the street and dying. The effects could not be seen on the surface. The food industry had too much money invested in hydrogenated oils for food preservation and preparation. The oils were cheap and profits higher. They had powerful lobbyists covering Congressional committees like an umbrella. It took record heart disease victims and other deadly health problems surfacing to go along with dedicated researchers persevering to bring the cause of this fatal ingredient in our food supply to light.

Sample Meal Plans Comparisons

BREAKFAST

Bad Choice   IF Rating

Eggs (Whole) 4 Oz	-170
Bacon (Pan Fried) 3 Oz	-36
Blueberry Muffin (1 Muffin)	<u>-75</u>
	-281

Good Choice

Eggs (Whole) 4 Oz	-170
Pan Fried Bacon (3 Oz)	-36
Hot Chili Peppers (1/2 Cup)	1,024
Red Grapefruit (1/2 Fruit)	<u>10</u>
	828

Bad Choice

Eggs (Whole) 4 Oz	-170
Ham Spiral Cut Roasted (3 Oz)	-32
English Muffin Mixed Grain (1 Muffin)	<u>-39</u>
	-241

Good Choice

Scrambled Egg Substitutes	20
Cayenne Pepper (1/2 Tsp)	254
Polish Sausage (Pork)	19
Red Grapefruit (1/2 Fruit)	<u>10</u>
	303

Bad Choice	IF Rating
Eggs Whites (6 Oz)	-6
Turkey Bacon (3 Oz)	-206
French Toast w/o Syrup	<u>-30</u>
	-242

Good Choice	
Omelette Egg Whites (6 Oz)	-6
Jalapeno Raw (1/2 Cup)	825
Ham Slice Extra Lean	2
Fat Free Mozzarella	<u>20</u>
	841

LUNCH OR DINNER

Bad Choice	IF Rating
Roasted Chicken Breast	-25
Kidney Beans (Canned)	-66
Beets (Canned)	<u>-6</u>
	-97

Good Choice	
Roasted Chicken Breast	-25
Sweet Potato Baked	189
Asparagus Cooked	<u>38</u>
	202

Bad Choice	
Chicken Wings Roasted	-56
Brown Rice	-143
Turnip Greens	<u>-1</u>
	-200

Good Choice	
Chicken Wings Roasted	-56
Broccoli Cooked	60
Butternut Squash Baked	<u>91</u>
	95

Bad Choice	IF Rating
Deer Loin Roasted	-99
Corn on the Cobb	-111
Black-eyed Peas (Canned w/ Pork)	<u>-86</u>
	-296

Good Choice	
Deer Loin Roasted	-99
Spinach Cooked	224
Carrots Cooked	<u>130</u>
	255

Bad Choice	
Pork Top Loin Broiled	-18
Baked Potato w/ Skin (White)	-47
Pinto Beans (Canned)	<u>-87</u>
	-152

Good Choice	
Pork Top Sirloin Broiled	-18
Mustard Greens Cooked	172
Okra Cooked	<u>10</u>
	164

The Worst Choices

Starchy Vegetables   **IF Rating**

    Pumpkin (Canned) — -68

    Corn on the Cobb — -111

        Cooked — -76

        Creamed Canned — -56

    Potato-Mashed — -69

        Hash Brown — -93

Non-Starchy Vegetables

    None

Fruits

    Blueberries Dried/Sweetened — -120

        Heavy Syrup — -70

        Syrup Drained — -65

    Blackberries Heavy Syrup — -65

    Boysenberries Heavy Syrup — -65

    Peaches Dried — -76

    Banana Chips Dried — -132

    Pineapple Frozen Sweet — -64

    Plums Heavy Syrup — -70

    Raisins — -135

        Seedless — -135

    Cherries Maraschino — -122

        Frozen Sweet — -76

        Tart Dried/Sweet — -143

	IF Ratings
Sweet Heavy Syrup	-64
Sour Heavy Syrup	-71
Sour Light Syrup	-63
Pears Dried	-114
Raspberries Frozen Sweet	-64
Heavy Syrup	-65
Prunes Dried	-91
Stewed	-82
Stewed w/ Sugar	-114
Cranberries Dried/Sweetened	-98
Papaya Heavy Syrup/Drained	-215

White Rice

Long Grain Cooked	-153
Instant Cooked	-131
Medium Grain Cooked	-184
Short Grain Cooked	-188

Brown Rice

Long Grain Cooked	-143
Medium Grain Cooked	-162

Noodles

Chow Mein	-91
Egg Cooked	-102
Rice Cooked	-150

Spaghetti	IF Rating
White Cooked	-124
Whole Wheat Cooked	-82
Spinach Cooked	-120

Oils

Coconut	-115
Cotton Seed	-94
Palm Kernel	-99
Poppy Seed	-78
Safflower High Linoleic	-91
Sunflower Linoleic	-77
Grapeseed	-87

Nuts

Sunflower Seeds Oil-Roasted	-63
Chestnuts Roasted	-70

Flour (All Averages -180)

Best Bets

Peanut Defatted	-1
Whole Wheat	-89
Oat	-103
Buckwheat	-100
Sesame Seed	-68
Soy Full Fat	-23
Low Fat	-7

Sugar (However GL is outrageous @ 150)   IF Rating
    Brown   -77
    Granulated   -63

Yogurt (No Good Choices)
    Check back of book under (Bad Guys) IF Ratings

Granola (Surprisingly, No Good Choices)
    Check back of book under (Bad Guys) IF Ratings

Milk
    See back of book under (Bad Guys) IF Ratings

Bread
    Sticks Plain   -80
    Crumbs   -91
    Sourdough   -261

Muffins
    Blueberry   -75

Rolls & Biscuits
    Cinnamon   -70
    Brown & Serve   -61
    Biscuits/Mix   -61
    Refrigerated Dough   -62
        Reduced Fat   -60

Dressings (All are below -50)
    Eat what you like

Cookies (No Good Choices)
Check back of book under (Bad Guys) IF Ratings

Ice Cream & Other Desserts (No Good Choices)
Check back of book under (Bad Guys) IF Ratings

Meat	IF Rating
Beef Heart Simmered	-168
Liver Braised	-233
Pan Fried	-143
Chicken Thigh Batter Fried	-76
Fried	-89
Stewed	-69
Wings Batter Fried	-80
Fried	-93
Stewed	-72
Leg Batter Fried	-73
Fried	-79
Stewed	-67
Chicken Heart Simmered	-502
Giblets Fried	-259
Simmered	-152
Liver Pan Fried	-272
Simmered	-274
Drumstick Batter Fried	-70
Fried	-74
Dark Meat Fried w/o Skin	-97
Roasted w/o Skin	-78

	IF Rating
Stewed w/o Skin	-71
Cornish Hens Roasted	-128
Roasted w/o Skin	-128
Pork Ground 72% Lean Cooked	-68
Spareribs Roasted	-67
Bacon Baked	-64
Bacon Microwaved	-91
Turkey Bacon	-206
Country Style Ham	-78
Deer Loin Roasted	-99
Ground Browned	-60
Elk Roasted	-77
Lamb Ribs Broiled	-77
Turkey Breast Roasted	-104
Giblets Simmered	-136
Ground Cooked	-80
Heart Simmered	-201
Liver Simmered	-184
Leg Roasted	-162
Smoked Turkey	-136
Wing Roasted	-102
Veal Loin Braised	-92
Roasted	-71
Liver Braised	-138
Pan Fried	-160
Rib Braised	-63

	IF Rating
Shoulder	-64
Sirloin Braised	-63

Eggs

Chicken Whole	-85
Yolk	-182
Goose	-126
Duck	-147

Beans (Have much nutrition)

Check back of book under (Bad Guys) IF Ratings

The Great Equalizers

The following pages list the outstanding anti-inflammatory foods, illustrating their impact upon a meal dominated by pro-inflammatory ones. There are plenty of pro-inflammatory whole foods we all love to eat which possess numerous important nutrients. With strategically placed **Great Equalizers,** we can enjoy them and still maintain meals rendering an anti-inflammatory rating. Keep in mind, one meal on the pro-inflammatory side of the scale doesn't place you in the stockade. The big picture is what matters; what side of the scale were you at the end of the day, week, or month. If you predominantly eat your meals from the anti-inflammatory side and avoid desserts and processed foods, you'll be in great shape.

Once you venture off into the center aisles of the grocery store, you are on your own. Enter at your own risk. There are very few items in that maze, you can afford to consume without inviting trouble from MSG, HFCS, and trans fats. These three killers are loaded with excitotoxins that cause deadly inflammation and obesity.

Even on the pro-inflammatory side (refer to the back of the book under Bad Guys IF Ratings), there are very few whole foods you should limit due to their inflammatory nature; their rating is low. Note, however, even if all the foods in a meal have extremely low IF ratings, it still renders a pro-inflammatory result. Consistent living on the pro-inflammatory side, no matter how low the rating, leaves the body in a state of inflammation – disease causing.

(The foods on the following pages are all IF Ratings)

FISH (3 Oz)

Striped Bass (Baked)	422
Blue Fish (Baked)	439
Flounder (Baked or Grilled)	204
Anchovy (Canned in Oil)	871
White Fish (Baked)	422
Halibut (Cold Water)	102
Salmon (Wild/Baked)	489
Salmon (Chinook/Baked)	582
Salmon (Canned)	444
Salmon (Sockeye/Baked)	493
Sardines (Atlantic)	435
Sardines (Pacific)	344
Swordfish (Baked)	349
Sea Bass (Baked)	344
Roe (Baked)	1,040
All Oysters	250-300
Mackerel (Atlantic/Baked)	510
Mackerel (Spanish/Baked)	395
Mackerel (Pacific/Baked)	683
Mackerel (Canned)	465
Rainbow Trout Wild (Baked)	308
Tuna Bluefin (Baked)	593
Tuna White (Canned in Water)	344

Note: Farm raised fish are often pro-inflammatory due to their diet being grain instead of algae and small fish.

Vegetables

- Spinach
  - Canned — 241
  - Cooked — 224
  - Frozen/Cooked — 187
- Dandelion Greens
  - Cooked — 131
  - Raw — 150
- Turnip Greens/Cooked — 238
- Mustard Greens/Cooked — 172
- Sweet Potato/Baked — 189
- Swiss Chard/Cooked — 121
- Kale
  - Cooked — 112
  - Frozen/Cooked — 213
- Broccoli/Cooked — 60
- Collards/Cooked — 159
- Carrots
  - Cooked — 130
  - Raw — 98
- Onions
  - Cooked — 240
  - Frozen/Cooked — 301
  - Raw — 292
  - Sweet Raw — 299

Seasonings

Cayenne (1/2 Tsp)	254
Ginger Root (1 Tbsp)	387
Ground Ginger Root (1/2 Tsp)	348
Garlic Raw (1 Tbsp)	215
Garlic Powder (1 Tbsp)	468
Turmeric (1 Tsp)	338

Chili Peppers (1/2 Cup)

Banana Raw	654
Hot Raw	1,024
Hot Sundried	1,366
Hungarian Raw	659
Jalapeno Canned	479
Jalapeno Raw	825
Serrano Raw	1,556
Green Canned	551
Hot Canned	701

Spreads

Almond Butter (1/4 Cup)	100
Peanut Butter w/ Omega 3 (2 Tbsp)	91

Bad Meals Saved by the Great Equalizer Designated by an *

Salmon (Wild/Baked)	489*
Corn on the Cobb	-111
White Baked Potato	-47
Chocolate Ice Cream (1/2 Cup)	<u>-83</u>
	248
Halibut (Cold Water)	497*
Rice Noodles	-150
Blackeyed Peas (Canned)	-86
Cornbread (2 Oz)	<u>-158</u>
	103
Rainbow Trout	308*
Garbanzo (Chick Peas)	-82
Bread Multi-Grain (1 Slice)	-34
Yogurt/Greek Berry (Chobani)	<u>-108</u>
	84
Pan Fried Liver (3 Oz)	-143
Turnip Greens Cooked	238*
Onions Cooked	240*
White Potato Baked	<u>-47</u>
	288

Pan Fried Liver	-143
Onions Cooked	240*
Brown Rice Cooked	-143
Spinach Cooked	<u>224*</u>
	178
Roasted Turkey Leg	-162
White Rice Cooked	-182
White Bread (2 Slices)	-106
Almond Butter	100*
Mustard Greens Cooked	172*
Green Chili Peppers Canned	<u>551*</u>
	373
T-Bone Steak Broiled (6 Oz)	-36
Lima Beans (Cooked)	-45
Carrots Cooked	<u>130*</u>
	49

Blenderize Your Vegetables

According to Dr. Russell Blaylock, a renowned neurosurgeon, health practitioner, author, and lecturer, one should try blenderizing their vegetables. The blender can do a much better job of tearing down the cell walls of the vegetables than your teeth ever dreamed of doing.

In his January 2009 newsletter, Dr. Blaylock says, "Drinking a cup of blenderized vegetable juice is the equivalent to eating eight to ten servings of raw fruits and vegetables. It's estimated that the body absorbs only about 30 percent of nutrients from eating raw, chewed vegetables. Blenderized vegetables are absorbed at a rate of 90 percent."

The following vegetables are important to your blending experience:

- Asparagus
- Carrots
- Spinach
- Broccoli
- Grape Tomatoes
- Cucumbers
- Kale
- Red Cabbage
- Collard Greens
- Cauliflower
- Brussels Sprouts
- Celery
- Parsley

Personally, none of these vegetables thrill my taste buds. However, they have proven to be a powerful force toward preventing a number of cancers. They contain flavonoids that are powerful antioxidants and have anti-inflammatory properties. This is the reason, I even allow them to grace my ever resistant lips. However, you can make a blended recipe bearable.

My recipe is:

- Frozen Strawberries (creates coldness)
- One Banana (cut into small pieces)
- Asparagus
- Broccoli
- Spinach
- Grape Tomatoes
- Carrots

I then pour 20-24 ounces of water down the blender's throat, secure the lid and hit the start button. My Ninja Professional 1000 watt guy then turns everything into liquid; makes 9 cups. I drink 3 cups all at once per day, placing the rest in the fridge, container and all. The three-cup concoction gives me 30 servings of raw fruits and vegetables for each of three days. A nutritionist explained the "stuff" will keep up to 10 days.

Now the pressure is off in terms of getting the proper amounts of fruits and "good" vegetables. I can then concentrate on lean meats and fish while tossing in another vegetable or two at mealtime. The vegetables will also be of the anti-inflammatory variety. We all need at least one starch per day, so a baked sweet potato will more than cover that. Take a peek at its anti-inflammatory rating!

In the beginning, I included 1-2 scoops of Dave Draper's Bomber Blend protein and a scoop of milled flax seed. This witch's brew had an algae-looking film on top. So horrible looking, I named it "pond scum." I suffered the gag reflex with every gulp! After removing the two ingredients I just mentioned, the solution was nice 'n liquidy. Not all that bad, now.

But, for those of you who like eating these vegetables, you may love the blenderized version. It certainly is convenient and the body loves it. My wife, Janel, loves those vegetables, but cannot block out the initial appearance of "pond scum."

If I can do this, so can you.

It's kind of fun to do the impossible.
- *Walt Disney*

Glycemic Load

The **glycemic load (GL)** of each food is a number that estimates how much and how fast that food will raise a person's blood glucose level and how quickly the body will use it up. The GL accounts for how much carbohydrate is in the food, excluding fiber.

Originally, the **glycemic index (GI)** was invented in 1981 by Dr. Thomas Wolever and Dr. David Jenkins at the University of Toronto. It measured how quickly a carbohydrate food would raise the blood-glucose level. It did not take into account just how much of a carbohydrate food was fiber. Some carbohydrate foods are mostly fiber in content, so the actual blood-glucose levels were not that much an effect on blood-glucose. For example, watermelon has a high glycemic index number of 72, but with its higher fiber content, its GL rating is a low 3.6; not much sugar (glucose impact).

This is where the **glycemic load**, developed by Harvard researchers, became the standard.

GL Ratings
10 & Below – Good
11-19 – Acceptable
20 & Above – Avoid

You will discover all the foods from the anti-inflammatory list, with few exceptions, will fall in the "good" range, and none in the "avoid" range. But keep in mind, even amongst the pro-inflammatory foods, it's the processed and packaged foods that are the worst offenders.

If you are a diabetic, obese, or just want to lose weight, stay in the 10 and below range. When your blood glucose spikes high and quickly, it tumbles quickly, actually falling below the level prior to eating that food. With the lower glucose level, you get hungry again and eat. Can we say that obesity begins with these foods? With the lower GL number, the body takes longer to process a food into glucose, thereby utilizing it longer. This enables a more steady glucose level causing less desire to eat.

You must be fit to give before you can be fit to receive.
- James Stephens

ANTI-INFLAMMATORY FOODS (GOOD GUYS)

"IF" RATINGS

- Beef
- Pork
- Fish
- Ham
- Duck
- Bison
- Rabbit
- Deer
- Elk
- Lamb
- Cheese
- Fruits
- Fruit Juices
- Nuts
- Non-Starchy Vegetables
- Starchy Vegetables
- Cereals & Flour
- Peppers
- Chili Peppers
- Spreads
- Seasonings/Roots/Sweeteners
- Oils

IF Rating Scale
1 to 100 … Mildly Anti-Inflammatory
100 to 500 … Moderately Anti-Inflammatory
501 & Over … Strongly Anti-Inflammatory

BEEF
IF ONLY (3 Oz)

	IF
Arm Pot Roast	
Braised	31
Raw	11
Blade Roast	
Braised	27
Raw	10
Bottom Round	
Raw	17
Roasted	10
Brisket	
Flat Half Raw	4
Braised	29
Point Half Raw	19
Braised	23
Whole Raw	8
Braised	15
Tri-Tip Roast	
Raw	5
Roasted	10
Eye of Round	
Raw	23
Roasted	23
Inside Skirt Steak	
Broiled	25

Tip Round | IF
Raw | 17
Roasted | 21

Ground
70% Lean Baked | 3
Broiled | 1
Brown | 3

Flanked Steak
Raw | 8
Browned | 10

Rib
Large End Raw | 3
Broiled | 2
Roasted | 17
Small End Raw | 6
Broiled | 2
Roasted | 23

Rump Steak
Grilled | 13
Strip Steaks Raw | 24

Shoulder Roast
Roasted | 26

Shoulder Steak
Braised | 8

Tenderloin
Raw | 8
Broiled | 8

	IF
Top Round Steak	
Raw	24
Broiled	27
Top Sirloin Steak	
Raw	16
Broiled	13
Top Loin Steak	
Raw	12
Broiled	7
Top Blade Steak	
Grilled	10
Top Blade Roast	
Broiled	27
Corned Beef Brisket	
Cooked	47
Raw	39

PORK
IF ONLY (3 Oz)

	IF
Tenderloin	
Broiled	9
Loin	
Whole Braised	6
Polish Sausage	
Pork	19
Pork Smoke	17
Canadian Bacon	
Grilled	3
Pork Bologna	
3 Oz	17

ALL FISH
IF ONLY (3 Oz)

Fish	IF
Grouper (Baked)	85
Bass (Fresh Water Raw)	133
Bass (Fresh Water Baked)	169
Bass (Striped Baked)	422
Bass (Striped Raw)	329
Bluefish (Baked)	439
Bluefish (Raw)	343
Caviar (Black & Red)	2,204
Catfish	
Breaded & Fried	43
Farmed & Baked	10
Farmed & Raw	8
Wild & Baked	38
Wild & Raw	32
Cisco (Raw)	106
Cisco (Smoked)	448
Cod	
Atlantic (Baked)	69
Atlantic (Canned)	69
Atlantic (Dried & Salted)	225
Atlantic (Raw)	80
Pacific (Baked)	78
Pacific (Raw)	64

	IF
Octopus	
Raw	67
Steamed	143
Anchovy	
Canned in oil-drained	871
Raw	595
Perch	
Baked	89
Raw	70
Clams	
Breaded-Fried	45
Canned-Drained	82
Raw	44
Steamed	166
Crabs	
Cakes	137
Blue (Canned)	87
Blue (Raw)	114
Blue (Steamed)	204
Dungeness (Raw)	158
Dungeness (Steamed)	204
Crayfish	
Farmed (Raw)	43
Farmed (Steamed)	43
Wild (Raw)	52
Wild (Steamed)	58

	IF
Croaker	
Atlantic (Breaded-Fried)	11
Atlantic (Raw)	40
Cutter fish	
Raw	56
Steamed	125
Drum	
Freshwater (Baked)	48
Freshwater (Raw)	38
King (Raw)	60
Steamed	197
Queen (Raw)	169
Steamed	212
White Fish	
Smoked	96
Baked	422
Raw	330
Whiting	
Baked	222
Raw	51
Fish Sticks	
Frozen	61
Fish Oil (1 Tbsp)	
Cod Liver	1061
Herring	688
Menhaden	1240
Salmon	1944

	IF
Sardine	1107
Halibut	
Baked	124
Greenland (Baked)	497
Greenland (Raw)	388
Raw	102
Herring	
Atlantic (Baked)	796
Atlantic (Kippered)	855
Atlantic (Pickled)	641
Atlantic (Raw)	624
Pacific (Baked)	814
Pacific (Raw)	638
Lobster	
Northern (Raw)	102
Northern (Steamed)	117
Spiny (Raw)	49
Spiny (Steamed)	67
Mackerel	
Atlantic (Baked)	510
Atlantic (Raw)	810
Canned & Drained	465
King (Baked)	214
King (Raw)	169
Pacific & Jack (Baked)	683
Pacific & Jack (Raw)	534

	IF
Salted	1663
Spanish (Baked)	395
Spanish (Raw)	414
Mullet	
Striped (Baked)	83
Striped (Raw)	75
Ocean Perch	
Baked	123
Raw	102
Oysters	
Canned	254
Eastern (Breaded & Fried)	246
Eastern (Farmed & Baked)	271
Eastern (Wild & Baked)	290
Eastern (Wild & Raw)	220
Eastern (Wild & Steamed)	345
Pacific (Raw)	332
Pacific (Steamed)	673
Pollock	
Atlantic (Baked)	223
Atlantic (Raw)	174
Walleye (Baked)	210
Walleye (Raw)	74
Rockfish	
Pacific (Baked)	177
Pacific (Raw)	147

	IF
Roe	
Baked	1040
Raw	813
Sablefish	
Baked	681
Raw	532
Smoked	702
Salmon	
Atlantic (Farmed & Baked)	848
Raw	725
Wild & Baked	489
Wild & Raw	383
Chinook (Baked)	582
Raw	689
Smoked	210
Chum (Baked)	330
Canned & Drained	444
Coho (Farmed & Baked)	454
Raw	421
Wild & Baked	439
Wild & Raw	354
Wild & Steamed	446
Pink (Baked)	268
Canned	407
Canned & Drained	442
Raw	223
Sockeye (Baked)	493

	IF
Canned & Drained	516
Raw	415
Sardines	
Atlantic (oil, drained)	435
Pacific (Tomato sauce-drained)	344
Scallops	
Bay & Sea (Steamed)	61
Breaded & (Fried)	42
Raw	30
Sea Bass	
Baked	344
Raw	262
Sea Trout	
Baked	14
Raw	11
Shark	
Batter-dipped & Fried	201
Raw	276
Shrimp	
Breaded & Fried	28
Canned	219
Raw	35
Steamed	76
Snapper	
Baked	129
Raw	113

	IF
Rainbow Smelt	
Baked	334
Raw	261
Squid	
Fried	216
Raw	201
Sturgeon	
Baked	107
Raw	84
Smoked	58
White Sucker	
Baked	152
Raw	118
Swordfish	
Baked	349
Raw	293
Tilapia	
Baked	63
Raw	50
Tilefish	
Baked	274
Raw	145
Trout	
Baked	209
Raw	164
Flounder	
Baked or Grilled	204

	IF
Rainbow Trout	
Farmed (Baked)	332
Farmed (Raw)	279
Wild (Baked)	308
Wild (Raw)	161
Tuna	
Bluefin Baked	593
Bluefin Raw	464
White in water	344
White in oil-drained	131
Yellowfin Baked	111
Yellowfin Raw	93
Light in oil-drained	106
Light in water-drained	110

HAM
IF ONLY (3 OZ)

Ham	**IF**
Canned	29
Slice Extra Lean	2
Steak	32
Ham & Cheese Loaf	16

DUCK
IF ONLY (3 OZ)

	IF
Meat Roasted	17
Meat & Skin Roasted	26
Meat & Skin Raw	31

BISON
IF ONLY (3 OZ)

	IF
Ground	
Cooked	2
Raw	19
Ribeye	
Broiled	21
Raw	27
Shoulder Roast	
Raw	25
Roasted	33
Top Round	
Broiled	23
Raw	26
Top Sirloin	
Broiled	22
Raw	29

RABBIT
IF ONLY (3 OZ)

	IF
Wild	
Raw	4
Stewed	22

DEER
IF ONLY (3 OZ)

	IF
Tenderloin Broiled	1
Top Round Broiled	2

ELK
IF ONLY (3 OZ)

	IF
Round Broiled	5

LAMB
IF ONLY (3 OZ)

Domestic Foreshank	IF
Braised	3
Quarters Cooked	175

CHEESE
(1 Cup)

	IF	GL
Non-Fat Swiss	20	4
Fat Free Mozzarella	20	2
Fat Free Mozzarella (Shredded)	20	2

FRUITS
IF (1/2 Cup) GL (1 Cup)

	IF	GL
Apricots		
Fresh	2	6
Mango		
Fresh	4	8
Kiwi		
Fresh	17	8
Blackberries		
Fresh	4	4
Cantaloupe		
Fresh	37	5
Orange		
Fresh	5	5
W/Peel	3	8
Pineapple		
Fresh	32	6
Raspberries		
Fresh	0	3
Red/Pink Grapefruit		
Fresh	9	7
White Grapefruit		
Fresh	1	5
Strawberries		
Fresh	14	3
Frozen (unsweetened)	8	4

Acerola Cherries	IF	GL
Fresh	342	1
Fresh in juice	817	2
Cherries		
Sour Fresh	6	
Sweet Fresh	7	
Lemon		
Peel Fresh 1 Tbsp	2	
Fresh w/o Peel	9	4
Fresh w/Peel	14	3
Lime		
Fresh	3	1

FRUIT JUICES

Orange Juice	IF	GL
Fresh 1/2 cup	1	9 (1 Cup)
Orange Drink Canned	13	6
V-8 Splash (8 oz.)		
Berry Blend	142	2
Diet Berry Blend	26	0
Diet Fruit Medley	26	0
Diet Strawberry Kiwi	26	0
Diet Tropical Blend	26	0
Tropical Blend	14	2
V-8 Fusion (8 oz.)		
Acai	5	5

Lemon Juice	IF	GL
Juice Bottled (1/2 Cup)	8	1
Lemon Juice Fresh (1/2 Cup)	17	3
Lemonade from Mix 8 oz.	2	1
Sugar Free from Mix 8 oz.	3	0
Lime Juice		
Juice Bottled (1/2 Cup)	2	1
Fresh Juice (1/2 Cup)	7	3
Pineapple-Grapefruit 8 oz.	0	7
Carrot Juice		
Canned (1 Cup)	212	8

NUTS

Almonds (1 Cup)	IF	GL
Raw	64	0
Blanched	71	0
Dry-Roasted	66	0
Honey Roasted	71	0
Oil-Roasted	77	0
Cashews		
Raw (1 Oz)	20	3
Dry-Roasted (1 Cup)	27	15
Oil-Roasted (1 Cup)	25	11
Brazil Nuts		
Raw	170	

	IF	GL
Macadamia (1 Cup)		
Dry-Roasted	159	0
Raw	155	0
Pecans		
Dry-Roasted (1 Oz)	65	0
Oil-Roasted (1 Cup)	45	0
Raw (1 Cup)	46	0
Pistachios (1 Cup)		
Dry-Roasted	16	4
Raw	19	5
Peanuts (1 Cup)		
Dry-Roasted	27	0
Oil-Roasted	25	0
Raw	20	0
Flaxseed (1 Cup)		
Fresh	39	0
Sunflower Seeds (1 Cup)		
Raw	12	0
Hickory Nuts		
Raw (1 Cup)	30	
Mixed Nuts (1 Cup)		
Dry-Roasted	61	1
Oil-Roasted	37	0
Oil-Roasted/No Peanuts	177	0
Trail Mix w/Chocolate Chips, Salted Nuts	33	

NON-STARCHY VEGETABLES
IF (1/2 Cup) GL (1 Cup)

	IF	GL
Broccoli		
Cooked	60	8
Frozen/Cooked Chopped	39	3
Raw	26	3
Brussels Sprouts		
Cooked	40	5
Raw	30	3
Asparagus		
Canned	34	3
Cooked	38	2
Raw	21	3
Spinach		
Canned	241	2
Cooked	224	2
Raw	74	0
Frozen/Cooked	187	2
Cucumber		
Peeled	1	1
Raw	0	1
Dandelion Greens (1 Cup)		
Cooked	131	3
Raw	150	2

	IF	GL
Kale		
Cooked	112	3
Raw	0	3
Frozen/Cooked (10 Oz)	213	4
Beet Greens (1 Cup)		
Cooked	136	4
Raw	63	0
Lettuce (1 Leaf)		
Bibb	36	1
Green Leaf	42	0
Iceberg	6	1
Romaine	10	0
Red Leaf	34	0
Tomato		
Cooked (Red Ripe)	9	4
Raw (Red Ripe)	9	2
Green Raw	5	4
Sundried Oil	12	9
Turnip Greens		
Cooked	238	1
Raw	134	1
Watercress		
Raw	32	0
Zucchini		
Cooked	14	1
Frozen/Cooked (10 Oz)	2	3
Raw	0	

	IF	GL
Onions		
Cooked	240	8
Frozen/Cooked (10 Oz)	301	0
Raw	292	5
Sweet Raw	299	3
Okra		
Cooked	10	6
Frozen/Cooked (10 Oz)	15	6
Raw	9	3
Radish		
Oriental Cooked	2	1
Oriental Raw	5	3
Raw	4	1
Rhubarb		
Fresh	1	2
Frozen	3	1
Frozen/Cooked (1 Cup)	29	
Cabbage (1 Cup)		
Chinese Cooked	57	1
Raw	30	1
Green Cooked	23	2
Raw	10	2
Red Cooked	3	1
Raw	12	2
Savoy Cooked	0	3
Raw	13	2

	IF	GL
Cauliflower		
Cooked	9	1
Raw	13	2
Frozen/Cooked	12	1
Green/Cooked	11	2
Raw	9	2
Celery (1 Cup)		
Cooked	9	2
Raw	7	1
Collards		
Cooked	159	4
Frozen/Cooked (1 cup)	45	5
Raw (1 cup)	62	1
Green Beans		
Canned	3	3
Cooked	1	4
Frozen/Cooked (10 Oz)	1	3
Mustard Greens		
Cooked (1 Cup)	172	0
Frozen/Cooked (10 Oz)	59	1
Swiss Chard		
Cooked	121	4
Raw (1 cup)	88	1
Mushrooms		
Brown	6	1
Portabella	1	2
Portabella Grilled	0	3

	IF	GL
Parsley		
Dried (1 Tsp)	2	0
Fresh (1 Tbsp)	20	2 (1 Cup)
Sauerkraut		
Canned	4	2

STARCHY VEGETABLES
IF (1/2 Cup) GL (1 Cup)

	IF	GL
Pumpkin		
Canned	168	6
Cooked	49	3
Raw	49	3
Carrots		
Canned (1 Tbsp)	79	0
Cooked (1 Tbsp)	130	0
Frozen/Cooked (10 Oz)	90	2
Raw (1 Cup Chopped)	98	3
Baby Raw (1 Large)	78	0
Summer Squash		
Raw	20	2
Cooked	9	3
Winter Squash		
Raw	4	
Cooked	58	8
Butternut		
Raw		
Cooked	139	
Sweet Potato		
Baked	189	10
Canned	45	24
Raw	76	11

Green Peas

	IF	GL
Frozen/Cooked (10 Oz)	9	13

CEREALS
IF (1 Cup) GL (1 Cup)

	IF	GL
General Mills		
Total	43	14
Kelloggs		
All Bran Extra Fiber	4	12
All Bran Buds	50	6
Bran Flakes	9	13

FLOUR

	IF	GL
Baker's Yeast		
Compressed (1 Pc)	27	1 (1 Cake)
Dry (1 Tsp)	19	1 (1 Tbsp)

PEPPERS

	IF	GL
Black Ground		
(1/2 Tsp)	1	
Cayenne (1/2 Tsp)	254	0
Green Cooked (1/2 Cup)	25	3
Frozen	11	0

	IF	GL
Raw	24	2
Sauteed	43	0
Red Cooked	87	3
Frozen	32	2
Raw	39	3
Sautéed	61	1
White Ground (1/2 Tsp)	2	
Yellow Raw (1/2 Cup)	52	4

CHILI PEPPERS
IF (1/2 Cup) GL (1 Cup)

	IF	GL
Banana (Raw)	654	2
Hot (Raw)	1,024	2
Hot (Sun Dried)	1,366	8
Hungarian (Raw)	659	1
Jalapeno (Canned)	479	2
Jalapeno (Raw)	825	2
Serrano (Raw)	1,556	3
Green (Canned)	551	2
Hot (Canned)	701	2

SPREADS
IF (Varies)

	IF	GL
Almond Butter		
1/4 Cup	100	0
Peanut Butter (2 Tbsp)		
Crunchy	18	0
Smooth	10	0
w/ Omega 3	91	0
Sunflower Seed Butter		
1/4 Cup	252	1
Cashew Butter		
1/4 Cup	72	1
Smart Balance		
Omega Plus	33	
Smart Balance Regular	5	
Mayonnaise (1 Tbsp)		
Olive Oil Light	34	
Smart Balance Omega Plus	15	
Mustard (1 Tsp)		
Prepared	2	5
Ground 1/2 Tsp	4	

SEASONINGS/ROOTS/SWEETENERS

	IF	GL
Ginger		
Root (1 Tbsp)	387	0
Ground (1/2 Tsp)	348	2
Pimento		
Canned (1/2 Cup)	54	3
Sage		
Ground (1/2 Tsp)	1	0
Salt		
(1/2 Tsp)	0	0
Spearmint		
Dried or Fresh	0	0
Garlic		
Raw (1 Tbsp)	215	22 (1 Cup)
Powder (1/2 Tsp)	468	3 (1 Tbsp)
Turmeric		
(1/2 Tsp)	338	2
Thyme		
Dried (1 Tsp)	3	0
Fresh (1 Tbsp)	3	0
Taro		
Leaves Cooked (1/2 Cup)	7	3
Raw (1 Cup)	31	1
Shoots Cooked (1/2 Cup)	2	2
Raw	1	1

	IF	GL
Curry		
(1 Tsp)	116	1
Flaxseed		
(1/4 Cup)	26	0

OILS
IF (1 Tbsp) GL (1 Cup)

	IF	GL
Almond	64	0
Apricot Kernel	34	0
Avocado	68	0
Canola	80	0
Corn & Canola Blend	56	0
Enova	1	0
Flaxseed	13	0
Hazelnut	87	0
Olive	74	0
Safflower High Oleic	79	0
Sunflower High Oleic	101	0
Sardine	1,107	0

PRO-INFLAMMATORY FOODS (BAD GUYS)

- Fruits
- Fruit Juices
- Nuts
- Non-Starchy Vegetables
- Starchy Vegetables
- Beans (Member of Starch Group)
- Rice (Member of Starch Group)
- Noodles/Spaghetti (Member of Starch Group)
- Beef
- Chicken/Duck
- Eggs
- Pork
- Ham
- Deer
- Elk/Moose
- Lamb
- Turkey
- Veal
- Hot Dogs
- Milk & Cottage Cheese
- Cheese

- Yogurt
- Cereals (Hot & Cold)
- Flour
- Bread
- Rolls & Biscuits2
- Muffins
- Crackers
- Spreads
- Dressings
- Seasonings/Roots/Sweeteners
- Desserts
- Coconut
- Granola
- Oils
- Poor Fast Food Choices

IF Rating Scale
-1 to -100 – Mildly Inflammatory
-101 to -500 – Moderately Inflammatory
-500 & Over – Strongly Inflammatory

FRUITS
IF (1/2 Cup) GL (1 Cup)

	IF	GL
Blueberries		
Fresh	-15	6
Frozen Unsweetened	-8	4
Frozen Sweetened	-34	16
Heavy Syrup	-70	20
Syrup Drained	-65	19
Dried Sweetened	-120	
Wild Frozen	-3	1
Blackberries		
Frozen	-12	6
Heavy Syrup	-65	22
Raw		4
Boysenberries		
Frozen	-4	4
Heavy Syrup	-65	21
Banana		
Fresh	-38	18
Chips-Dried (1oz)	-132	23
Apple		
Peeled	-10	3
With Skin	-9	3
Dried 1/4 cup	-49	26
Applesauce sweetened	-41	15
Applesauce unsweetened	-15	5

	IF	GL
Peaches		
Fresh (1 Large)	-10	5
Dried 1/4 cup	-76	46
Frozen sweet	-28	22
Heavy Syrup	-54	17
In Juice	-22	8
Light Syrup	-30	10
Syrup-Drained	-39	14
Pineapple		
Frozen Sweet	-64	19
Heavy Syrup	-56	19
In Juice	-36	12
Juice-Drained	-25	8
Light Syrup	-26	9
Plums		
Fresh	-10	5
Heavy Syrup	-70	21
In Juice	-25	12
Light Syrup	-38	12
Syrup-Drained	-49	15
Raisins		
Golden 1/4 cup	-136	75
Seedless 1/4 cup	-135	75
Tangerines		
In Juice	-1	7
Light Syrup	-29	13
Drained	-3	5

Pears (1 Fruit)

	IF	GL
Anjou Green Fresh	-91	54
Anjou Green Fresh	-16	5
Red Fresh	-12	5
Asian Fresh	-7	2
Bartlett Fresh	-14	5
Bosc Fresh	-16	5
Dried 1/4 cup	-114	63
Heavy Syrup	-49	14
In Juice	-26	7
Light Syrup	-31	9
Syrup Drained	-36	10

Cherries

Frozen Sweet	-76	22
Maraschino	-122	1
Sour Fresh	-3	6
Sour Frozen	-9	5
Sour Heavy Syrup	-71	23
Sour In Juice	-8	6
Sour Light Syrup	-63	18
Sweet Fresh	-26	7
Sweet Heavy Syrup	-64	19
Sweet In Juice	-38	11
Sweet Light Syrup	-45	14
Sweet Syrup Drained	-43	13
Tart Dried-Sweet	-143	

	IF	GL
Raspberries		
Frozen Sweet	-64	22
Heavy Syrup	-65	21
Prunes		
Dried 1/4 cup	-91	54
Stewed	-82	25
Stewed w/sugar	-114	31
In Juice	-51	16
Watermelon		
Fresh	-3	3
Strawberries		
Frozen Sweet	-23	17
Grapefruit		
Canned in Juice	-6	7
Canned in Light Syrup	-33	13
Grapes		
Red or White		
(Green)	-30	1
Papaya		
Heavy Syrup Drained 1/2 cup	-215	20
In Juice Sweetened	-21	
Fresh Juice	-9	9
Cranberries		
Dried-Sweetened (1/4 cup)	-98	17 (1/3 Cup)
Fresh	-2	2

FRUIT JUICE
IF (1/2 Cup) GL (1 Cup)

	IF	GL
V-8 Splash Smoothies (8 Oz)		
Peach Mango	-37	2
Strawberry/Banana	-40	2
Tropical Colada	-40	9
Lemon Juice from Concentrate		
8 Oz	-33	2
Flavored Drink Mix (8 oz)	-5	11
Lemon-Lime Soda (8 oz)	-36	1
Grapefruit Juice		
Juice (1/2 cup)	-7	7
Fresh Juice (1/2 cup)	-3	7
Sweetened	-17	9
Prune Juice		
1/2 Cup	-51	16
Pineapple/Orange Juice		
8 oz	-63	13
Orange/Pineapple		
1/2 cup	-11	13
Apple Juice		
1/2 cup	-12	6
Grape Juice		
Pure	-30	12
Juice Canned	-34	12
Drink Canned	-40	10

Limeaide from Concentrate	IF	GL
8 oz	-56	1
Orange Juice Drink		
Canned (8 oz)	-46	5
Passion Fruit		
Purple Juice Fresh	-7	9
Yellow Juice Fresh	-24	13
Fresh	-18	2

NUTS
(1/4 Cup)

Walnuts	IF	GL
Black Raw	-35	0
English Raw	-34	0
Sunflower Seeds		
Dry-Roasted	-48	1
Oil-Roasted	-63	0
Sesame Seeds		
Hulled	-9	0
Unhulled	-5	0
Chestnuts		
Raw	-50	
Japanese		5
Chinese		7
European		7

	IF	GL
Boiled	-36	
Japanese		1
Chinese		5
European		4
Roasted	-70	
Japanese		8
Chinese		9
European		42
Peanuts		
Boiled	-5	0

NON-STARCHY VEGETABLES
IF (1/2 Cup) GL (1 Cup)

	IF	GL
Eggplant		
Cooked	-5	2
Raw	-2	1
Beets		
Canned	-6	3
Cooked	-9	3
Raw	-1	5
Harvard Canned	-47	
Pickled	-34	
Yellow Beans		
Canned	-2	1
Cooked	-3	4

Mushrooms	IF	GL
Brown Canned	-9	1
Enoki Raw	-4	0
Maitke Raw	-5	2
Oyster Raw	-5	5
Shitake Cooked	-5	7
Straw Canned	-2	4
White Raw	-3	2
Portabella Raw	-3	2
Rutabagas		
Cooked	-4	5
Raw	-3	4
Tomato		
Sundried (1/4 cup)	-16	12
Canned Crushed	-12	1
Canned in Sauce	-2	6
Canned Stewed	-9	6

STARCHY VEGETABLES
(1/2 Cup)

Pumpkin	IF	GL
Pre-Mix Canned	-64	6
Pie Spice (1 Tbsp)	-2	1
Seed Kernels Dried (1/4 Cup)	-68	2
Seeds (Whole Roasted) (1/4 Cup)	-28	22

	IF	GL
Corn		
On the Cobb	-111	6
Canned	-36	8
Cooked	-76	17
Cream Canned	-56	18
Frozen	-42	6
Raw	-58	11
Cornbread (1 oz)	-79	
Potato		
White Baked	-47	13
Baked w/o Skin	-40	6
Boiled w/o Skin	-44	26
Canned	-31	9
Raw	-32	2
Mashed	-69	16
Instant-Mashed	-52	98
Hash Browned	-93	6
Red Baked	-42	26
Raw	-32	2
Black-eyed Peas		
Canned w/Pork (1 cup)	-86	
Dried	-78	
Dried-Cooked (1 cup)	-19	
Green Peas		
Canned	-4	4
Cooked	-3	9

French Fries

	IF	GL
Frozen/Oven Baked	-51	8

BEANS: (MEMBERS OF THE STARCH GROUP)
IF (1 Cup) GL (1 Cup)

	IF	GL
Kidney Beans		
Canned (1 cup)	-66	15
Dried-Cooked	-60	15
Sprouted, Cooked, Boiled	-6	1
Lentils		
Cooked/Boiled	-15	13
Lima Beans		
Canned		14
Cooked	-45	14
Frozen/Cooked	-52	8
Large Dried Cooked (1 Cup)	-61	14
Raw	-29	48
Small Dried Cooked	-48	16
Navy Beans		
Canned (1 cup)	-108	21
Cooked (1 Cup)	-51	15
Sprouted, Cooked, Boiled		1
Pinto Beans		
Canned (1 Cup)	-87	14
Dried-Cooked (1 Cup)	-43	15

	IF	GL
Refried Beans		
Canned-Fat Free (1 Cup)	-74	12
Soy Beans		
Cooked	-13	
Dried-Cooked (1 Cup)	-44	
Dry-Roasted (1 Cup)	-72	
Roasted (1 Cup)	-83	
Fava Beans		
Canned (1 Cup)	-71	13
Raw	-34	10
Dried-Cooked	-54	13
Great Northern Beans		
Canned (1 Cup)	-111	22
Raw	-72	46
Dried-Cooked (1 Cup)	-55	13
Black Beans		
Raw	-115	57
Dried-Cooked	-47	14
Black Turtle Beans		
Canned (1 Cup)	-60	13
Raw	-118	41
Dried-Cooked	-80	19
Cow Peas		
Cooked	-14	
Dried	-69	
Dried-Cooked (1 Cup)	-54	
Frozen	-29	

	IF	GL
Raw	-12	
Garbanzo (Chickpeas)		
Canned (1 Cup)	-82	23
Dried	-83	52
Dried-Cooked (1 Cup)	-70	17
Parsnips		
Raw	-8	7
Cooked, Boiled	-86	4
Baked Beans	-65	
w/ Pork	-52	

RICE

	IF	GL
Brown		
Long Grain-Cooked (1 Cup)	-143	22
Medium Grain-Cooked (1 Cup)	-162	22
White		
Glutinous-Cooked (1 Cup)	-125	18
Long Grain-Cooked (1 Cup)	-153	22
Instant Cooked (1 Cup)	-131	
Medium Grain-Cooked (1 Cup)	-184	29
Short Grain-Cooked (1 Cup)	-188	30

NOODLES

	IF	GL
Chow Mein		
1 oz	-91	15 (1 Cup)
Egg (1 Cup)		
Cooked	-102	21
Rice (1 Cup)		
Cooked	-150	20
Spinach		
1 Cup	-56	

SPAGHETTI

	IF	GL
White Cooked (1 Cup)	-124	23
Spinach Cooked (1 Cup)	-120	20
Whole Wheat Cooked (1 Cup)	-82	15

BEEF
IF RATINGS ONLY (3 Oz)

Tongue
- Raw — -265
- Simmered — -17

Liver
- Braised — -233
- Pan Fried — -143
- Raw — -8

Kidney
- Simmered — -230
- Raw — -70

Heart
- Simmered — -168
- Raw — -103

Porterhouse Steak
- Broiled — -13
- Raw — -11

Rib Eye
- Broiled — -5

T-Bone Steak
- Broiled — -18
- Raw — -13

Tenderloin
- Roasted — -8

Top Round Roast
- Broiled — -1

Tripe

Raw	-26
Simmered	-53

Ground

70% Lean Raw	-6
80% Lean Raw	-5
Browned	-1
Broiled	-4
Baked	-4
90% Lean Raw	-6
Browned	-10
Broiled	-8
Baked	-7
95% Lean Raw	-6
Browned	-16
Broiled	-9
Baked	-4

Filet Mignon

Broiled	-26

Rump Steak

Raw	-9

Shoulder Medallion

Raw	-10
Grilled	-6

Top Blade Steak

Raw	-5

CHICKEN
IF RATINGS ONLY (3 Oz)

Chicken Breast
- Batter Fried — -48
- Fried — -43
- Raw — -19
- Roasted — -25
- Stewed — -24

Chicken Thigh
- Batter Fried — -76
- Fried — -89
- Raw — -84
- Roasted — -56
- Stewed — -69

Chicken Wings
- Batter Fried — -80
- Fried — -93
- Raw — -48
- Roasted — -56
- Stewed — -72

Chicken Leg
- Batter Fried — -73
- Fried — -79
- Raw — -82
- Roasted — -50
- Stewed — -67

Chicken Heart
Raw	-604
Simmered	-502

Chicken Gizzard
Raw	-47
Simmered	-50

Giblets
Fried	-259
Simmered	-152

Liver
Pate Canned	-5
Pan Fried	-272
Raw	-138
Simmered	-152

Drumstick
Batter Fried	-70
Fried	-74
Raw	-78
Roasted	-59
Stewed	-58

Dark Meat
Fried w/o Skin	-97
Raw w/o Skin	-50
Roasted w/o Skin	-78
Stewed w/o Skin	-71

Light Meat

Fried w/o Skin	-57
Raw w/o Skin	-24
Roasted w/o Skin	-33
Stewed w/o Skin	-27

Cornish Hens

Roasted	-128
Roasted w/o Skin	-115
Raw	-106
Raw w/o Skin	-102

DUCK
IF RATINGS ONLY (3 Oz)

Duckling Roasted	-31
Duck Liver Raw	-29

EGGS
IF RATINGS ONLY (2 Oz)

Chicken Egg

White	-2
Whole	-85
Yolk	-182
Turkey Egg	-56
Quail Egg	-55
Goose Egg	-126
Duck Egg	-147

PORK
IF RATINGS ONLY (3 Oz)

Chops
    Center Rib (Boneless)
        Braised   -12
        Broiled   -1
        Raw   -45
    Center Rib
        Braised   -54
        Broiled   -30
        Pan Fried   -58
        Raw   -18
    Sirloin
        Braised   -54
        Broiled   -45
        Raw   -14
    Top Loin (Boneless)
        Braised   -14
        Broiled   -18
        Pan Fried   -24
        Raw   -16

Ground Pork
    72% Lean
        Cooked   -68
        Raw   -62
    96% Lean

Cooked	-49
Raw	-35
Extra Lean Crumbles	-14
Lean	
Cooked	-49
Crumbles	-47
Raw	-52

Hocks

Pickled	-32

Loin

Whole Broiled	-2
Raw	-36
Roasted	-17

Ribs

Country Style	
Braised	-40
Raw	-16
Roasted	-46
Raw	-48
Roasted	-52
Spareribs	
Braised	-52
Raw	-474
Roasted	-64

Tenderloin

Raw	-20
Roasted	-16

Peppercorn Flavored	-17
Teriyaki Flavored	-20

Bacon

Grease (1 Tbsp)	-3
Raw	-90
Baked	-67
Microwaved	-91
Canadian-Uncooked	-29
Bacon Pan Fried	-36
Turkey Bacon	-206

HAM
IF RATINGS ONLY (3 Oz)

Country Style	-78
Honey Smoked	-16
Spiral Cut Roasted	-32
Turkey	-59
Water Added	-34

DEER
IF RATINGS ONLY (3 Oz)

Ground

Browned	-60
Raw	-49

Loin

Broiled	-4
Raw	-69
Roasted	-99

Shoulder Roast

Braised	-5

ELK
IF RATINGS ONLY (3 Oz)

Ground Browned	-50
Ground Raw	-50
Loin Broiled	-7
Raw	-65
Roasted	-77

MOOSE
IF RATINGS ONLY (3 Oz)

Raw	-45
Roasted	-50

LAMB
IF RATINGS ONLY (3 Oz)

Domestic Leg

Raw	-18
Roasted	-15

Domestic Foreshank
Raw	-5

Domestic Loin
Broiled	-29
Raw	-43
Roasted	-43

Domestic Rib
Broiled	-77
Raw	-73
Roasted	-53

Domestic Shoulder
Braised	-51
Broiled	-31
Raw	-44
Roasted	-43

Ground
Broiled	-23
Raw	-49

TURKEY
IF RATINGS ONLY (3 Oz)

Neck
Simmered w/o Skin	-54
Raw w/o Skin	-48

Breast
Deli-Sliced	-12

Raw	-54
Roasted	-104
Dark Meat	
Raw w/o Skin	-6
Roasted w/o Skin	-41
Giblets	
Raw	-121
Simmered	-136
Gizzard	
Raw	-49
Simmered	-43
Ground	
Cooked	-80
Raw	-63
Heart	
Raw	-153
Simmered	-201
Leg	
Raw	-98
Roasted	-162
Liver	
Raw	-123
Simmered	-184
Light Meat	
Raw w/o Skin	-2
Roasted w/o Skin	-8

Smoked Turkey
   3 Oz   -136
Wing
   Raw   -54
   Roasted   -103

VEAL
IF RATINGS ONLY (3 Oz)

Breast
   Boneless Braised   -42
   Boneless Raw   -33
Ground
   Broiled   -56
   Raw   -45
Kidneys
   Braised   -114
   Raw   -56
Leg
   Braised   -44
   Pan Fried Breaded   -63
   Pan Fried Not Breaded   -38
   Raw   -26
   Roasted   -32
Liver
   Braised   -138
   Pan Fried   -160

Raw	-132
Loin	
Braised	-92
Raw	-56
Roasted	-71
Rib	
Braised	-63
Raw	-75
Roasted	-42
Shank	
Braised	-42
Raw	-42
Shoulder Arm	
Braised	-39
Shoulder	
Braised	-53
Raw	-40
Roasted	-64
Sirloin	
Braised	-63
Raw	-37
Roasted	-52

HOT DOGS
IF RATINGS ONLY (3 Oz)

Chicken	-47
Pork	-18
Turkey	-48

MILK & COTTAGE CHEESE

	IF	GL
Buttermilk Whole		
(1 Cup)	-76	9
Chocolate (1 Cup)		
Reduced Fat 2%	-114	14
Whole	-109	13
Low Fat 1%	-109	13
Condensed Sweetened		
(2 Tbsp)	-98	100
Evaporated (1/2 Cup)		
Fat Free	-48	15 (1 Oz)
Whole	-70	2 (1 Oz)
Milk (1 Cup)		
Fat Free	-52	9
Low Fat - 1%	-60	9
Reduced Fat - 2%	-71	9
Whole	-74	9
Goat Milk		
(1 Cup)	-92	8

	IF	GL
Indian Buffalo	-127	9 (1 Cup)
Sheep Milk	-122	9 (1 Cup)
Chocolate Milkshake	-183	3 (1 Oz)
Vanilla Milkshake	-159	2 (1 Oz)
Soy Milk Chocolate		
Light	-67	21 (12 Oz)
Soy Milk Plain		
Light	-37	12 (12 Oz)
Soy Milk Vanilla		
Light	-47	17 (12 Oz)
Cottage Cheese (1/2 Cup)		
Creamed	-24	4 (4 Oz)
Fat Free	-23	6 (1 Cup)
Low Fat - 1%	-17	6 (1 Cup)
Reduced Fat - 2%	-21	7 (1 Cup)
Creamed w/Fruit	-24	8 (1 Cup)

CHEESE

Of all the 62 kinds of cheese currently on the market, all are on the **inflammatory** side of the scale with the exception of:

   Non-Fat Swiss

   Fat Free Mozzarella

   Fat Free Mozzarella Shredded

The 59 other forms of cheese have an average inflammatory rating of -32, with whole milk ricotta measuring a robust -62.

This section not only includes each one's GL rating, but more importantly with this product, included are fat grams and calories.

The findings will set you back on your heels.

CHEESE

	GL	Calories	Total Fat Grams
Mozzarella			
Nonfat	2 (1 Cup)	336	25
Nonfat	2 (1 Cup)	168	0
Low Fat	1 (1 Cup)	413	29
Low Sodium	4 (1 Cup)	370	23
Parmesan			
Shredded	0 (1 Tbsp)	21	1
Hard	0 (1 Cubic In.)	0	3
Low Sodium	2 (1 Cup)	456	30
Grated	2 (1 Cup)	431	29
American			
Pasteurized Low-fat	5 (1 Cup)	252	10
Pasteurized w/ Disodium Phosphate	1 (Cup)	525	44
Pasteurized wo/ Disodium Phosphate	0 (1 Cubic In.)	67	6
Swiss Cheese (Processed)			
Low Fat	5 (1 Cup)	238	7
Pasteurized w/ Disodium Phosphate	3	468	35
Pasteurized wo/			

	GL	Calories	Total Fat Grams
Disodium Phosphate	0	60	5
Swiss (Non-Processed)		502	37
Low Fat	3 (1 Cup)	236	7
Low Sodium	3 (1 Cup)	496	36
Blue Cheese	0 (1 Cubic In.)	60	5
Cheddar	1 (1 Cup)	532	44
Low Fat	3 (1 Cup)	228	9
Low Sodium	1 (1 Cup)	525	43
Colby	1 (1 Cup)	520	42
Low Fat	3 (1 Cup)	228	9
Low Sodium	1 (1 Cup)	525	43
Cheshire	1 (1 Oz)	108	9
Feta	4 (1 Cup)	396	32
Goat (Hard Type)	0 (1 Oz)	127	10
Semi-Soft	0 (1 Oz)	102	8
Soft	0 (1 Oz)	75	6
Limburger	0 (1 Cup)	438	7
Mexican Cheese			
Queso Anejo	3 (1 Cup)	492	40
Queso Asadero	2 (1 Cup)	470	37
Queso Chihuahua	3 (1 Cup)	494	39
Monterey	1 (1 Cup)	492	40
Low Fat	1 (1 Cup)	413	29
Cheese Fondue	7 (1 Cup)	492	29
Cheese Roquefort	1 (1 Pack)	324	26
American Cheese Food			
Pasteurized Process w/ Di Phosphate	8 (1 Pack)	745	56
Pasteurized Process w/o Di Phosphate	4 (1 Cup)	373	28

	GL	Calories	Total Fat Grams
Nachos w/Cheese, Beans, Beef, Peppers	30 (6-8 Nachos)	569	31
Kraft Velveeta Pasteurized Process	1 (Oz)	85	6
Reduced Fat	2 (1 Oz)	62	3
Sargento Ultra-Thin			
Colby Jack	1 (3 Slices)	120	10
Cheddar	1 (3 Slices)	130	10
Borden Sharp Cheddar			
2% Milk	1 (1 Oz)	80	6
Provolone	2 (1 Cup)	463	35
Reduced Fat	1 (1 Slice)	77	5
Ricotta	7 (1 Cup)	428	32
Part Skim Milk	9 (1 Cup)	339	19
Romano	3 (5 Oz)	549	38
Cottage Cheese (1 Cup)			
(Large or Small Curd)			
Creamed	4	111	5
Creamed w/Fruit	8	219	9
1% Milk Fat	6	163	2
2% Milk Fat	7	194	6
Non-fat	6	104	0
Cream Cheese	2 (1 Cup)	794	79
Low Fat	11 (1 Cup)	482	37
Non-fat	1 (1 Oz)	39	0

YOGURT
(1 Cup)

	IF	GL
Fat Free Chocolate	-167	3
Fat Free Fruit	-145	21
Fat Free Plain	-56	11
Fat Free Vanilla	-60	1
Greek Berry		
(Chobani)	-108	
Low Fat Fruit	-151	23
Low Fat Low Sugar	-150	21
Low Fat Plain	-66	10
Lot Fat Vanilla	-107	17
Soy	-125	11
Whole Milk Plain	-72	8
Frozen Yogurt		
Chocolate	-66	19
Frozen Yogurt		
Fat Free, Sugar Free	-43	19

CEREALS
IF (1 Cup) GL (1 Cup)

Health Valley	IF	GL
Oat Bran Flakes	-115	12
Fiber 7 Flake	-110	13
Quaker		
Oat Bran	-43	1
Oat Bran Raw	-24	12
Oatmeal Squares	-104	27
Oatmeal Squares w/ Cinnamon	-110	29
Oatmeal Instant		
Flavored Prepared	-106	11
Oatmeal Instant Prepared	-62	13
Oatmeal Regular Prepared	-84	13
Oats Whole Grain (1/3 Cup)	-137	
Life	-64	16
Life Cinnamon	-28	16
Cream of Wheat		
Flavored Prepared	-136	14
Cream of Wheat		
Instant Prepared	-75	15
Cream of Wheat		
Instant Prepared	-75	15
Cream of Wheat		
Regular Prepared	-78	13

Nabisco	IF	GL
Cream of Rice Regular prepared	-78	11
General Mills		
Oatmeal Crisp w/ Almonds	-196	28
Oatmeal Crisp w/ Apple Cinnamon	-177	30
Oatmeal Crisp w/ Raisin	-224	32
Wheaties	-43	13
Wheaties Raisin Bran	-136	27
Cheerios	-27	12
Cheerios Apple Cinnamon	-86	17
Cheerios Frosted	-68	16
Cheerios Honey Nut	-62	13
Cheerios Multi-Grain	-51	15
Cheerios Yogurt Burst	-82	16
Corn Chex	-73	18
Corn Chex Frosted	-121	20
Chex Honey Nut	-147	20
Chex Multi-Grain	-69	23
Chex Rice	-55	17
Chex Wheat	-95	23
Cinnamon Grahams	-129	18
Cinnamon Toast Crunch	-91	16
Cinnamon Toast Crunch Reduced Sugar	-72	

	IF	GL
Cookie Crisp	-83	18
Fiber One (1/2 Cup)	-11	6
Honey Nut Clusters	-190	31
Golden Grahams	-116	18
Kellogg's		
Rice Krispies	-71	20
Raisin Bran	-143	12
Raisin Bran Crunch	-190	
Raisin Nut Bran	-191	26
Cocoa Krispies	-152	19
Cocoa Pebbles	-150	
Corn Flakes	-96	17
Corn Flakes Honey Crunch	-145	18
Corn Flakes Reduced Sodium	-141	17
Corn Pops	-102	20
Fruit Loops	-90	
Fruit Loops Reduced Sugar	-71	19
Frosted Flakes	-151	20
Frosted Flakes Reduced Sugar	-128	20
Frosted Rice Krispies	-152	20
Fruit Harvest w/Berries	-125	17
Honey Smacks	-123	17
Apple Jacks	-90	21

	IF	GL
Crispix	-65	18
Crispy Brown Rice	-130	18
Cracklin' Oak Bran	-147	19
Coco Pops		20
Mini-Wheats Frosted w/ Strawberries		29
Special K	-34	14
All Bran		8
Post		
Shredded Wheat (1 Cup)	-156	26
Shredded Wheat n'Bran Spoon size	-188	24
Shredded Wheat Honey Nut	-157	
Grape Nuts (1/2 Cup)	-152	16
Honey Bunches of Oats	-74	17
Honey Bunches of		
Oats Honey Roasted	-91	16
Honeycombs	-119	18
Alpha Bits	-64	18
Alpha Bits w/Marshmallows	-118	18
Fruity Pebbles	-138	17
Golden Crisp	-117	8
Banana Nut Crunch	-121	27
Malt-o-Meal (Instant)		
Puffed Rice	-70	10
Puffed Wheat	-67	7
Puffed Raisin Bran	-75	25
High Fiber Bran Flakes	-24	13

	IF	GL
Blueberry Muffin Tops	-136	16
Cinnamon Toasters	-110	15
Apple Cinnamon	-106	16
Frosted Flakes	-120	20
Honey Nut Toasty O's	-78	16
Golden Puffs	-115	24

FLOUR
IF (1/3 Cup) GL (1 Cup)

	IF	GL
Rice		
Brown	-198	81
White	-220	91
Oat		
1/3 Cup	-103	11 (1 Oz)
Soy		
Full Fat	-23	11
Low Fat	-7	9
Sesame Seed		
1/3 Cup	-68	3 (1 Oz)
Corn Flour		
Degermed	-186	77 (1 Cup)
Masa White	-132	
Masa White Enriched	-119	51
Masa Yellow Enriched	-118	61
White Whole Grain	-135	56

	IF	GL
Yellow Whole Grain	-134	56
Cornmeal		
Degermed White	-198	88
Degermed Yellow	-197	88
Self-Rising White	-146	78
Self-Rising Yellow	-146	78
Whole Grain White	-140	58
Whole Grain Yellow	-139	58
Corn Starch	-216	
Buckwheat		
Flour	-100	44
Barley		
Flour	-139	62
Malt Flour	-173	78
Hulled	-140	65
Pearled Cooked (1 Cup)	-127	19
Pearled Raw	-175	80
White Flour		
All Purposed Bleached	-141	66
All Purpose Self-Rising	-134	64
All Purpose Unbleached	-141	66
Flour Bread	-142	68
Flour Cake	-174	76
Whole Wheat		
Flour	-89	44

	IF	GL
Peanut Flour		
Defatted	-1	6
Potato Flour		
Defatted		88

BREAD
IF (1 Slice) GL (1 Slice)

	IF	GL
Multi-Grain	-34	5
Oatmeal	-40	7
Reduced Calorie	-50	7
Banana	-70	19
Oat Bran	-32	6
Reduced Calorie	-22	6
Raisin	-47	9
Pumpernickel	-40	6
Pita (Whole Wheat)	-47	17
Italian	-49	9
Rye	-41	8
Reduced Calorie	-19	3
Rice Bran	-34	6
Cracked Wheat	-42	1
Bread Sticks Plain	-80	21
Bread Crumbs	-91	51
Sourdough	-261	
Wheat	-49	5
Bran	-39	9

	IF	GL
White	-53	14
Whole Wheat	-38	5
Reduced Calorie	-22	
Wheat Germ	-47	8
Croutons	-84	14

French Toast

	IF	GL
Frozen	-38	10
Homemade	-30	9

ROLLS & BUSCUITS
IF (1 Oz) GL (1 Roll or Biscuit)

	IF	GL
Cinnamon	-70	24
Egg Roll	-49	11
French	-48	11
Hamburger (Low Calorie)	-26	7
Hot Dog (Low Calorie)	-26	7
Hamburger (Multi-Grain)	-33	10
Hot Dog (Multi-Grain)	-33	10
Hamburger (White)	-55	13
Hot Dog (White)	-55	13
Kaiser	-56	18
Oat Bran	-32	7
Pumpernickel	-51	10
Rye	-51	13

	IF	GL
Wheat	-39	7
White (Brown & Serve)	-61	26
Whole Wheat	-44	11
Biscuits from Mix	-61	8
Multi-Grain	-54	
Refrigerated Dough	-62	14
Reduced Fat	-60	

MUFFINS
IF (1 Oz) GL (1 Muffin)

	IF	GL
Blueberry	-75	10
Blueberry Low Fat	-59	13
Corn	-63	5
Corn from Mix	-53	8
Oat Bran	-48	4
English Muffin Cinnamon Raisin	-48	16
English Muffin Mixed Grain	-43	17
English Muffin Plain	-53	16
English Muffin Wheat	-39	13
English Muffin Whole Wheat	-26	12

CRACKERS
IF (1 Oz) GL (Varies)

	IF	GL
Ritz	-94	6 (5 Crackers)
Low Sodium	-77	
Cheese Filling	-64	6
Peanut Butter Filling	-56	5
Rye	-60	20 (1 Cup)
Crispbread	-81	24 (1 Cup)
Cheese Filling	-58	5 (1/2 Oz)
Saltine	-106	3 (2 Crackers)
Fat Free	-114	9 (3 Crackers)
Reduced Fat	-95	
Wheat w/ Cheese	-67	6 (1/2 Oz)
w/ Peanut Butter	-54	5 (1/2 Oz)
Triscuit	-78	33 (1 Cup)
Reduced Fat	-88	
Wheat Thins	-88	33 (1 Cup)
Low Sodium	-59	33 (1 Cup)
Cheese Crackers	-89	14 (6 Crac.)
w/Peanut butter	-52	3 (6 Crac.)
Matzo Plain	-119	17 (1 Crac.)
White Wheat	-67	11 (1 Crac.)
Egg & Onion	-101	14 (1 Crac.)
Egg	-114	15 (1 Crac.)
Melba Toast	-91	15 (1 Cup)

	IF	GL
Rye & Pumpernickel	-90	7 (1/2 Oz)
Wheat	-80	7 (1/2 Oz)

SPREADS

Butter (1 Tbsp)

	IF	GL
Light	-25	0 (1 Oz)
Salted	-44	0 (1 Cup)
Unsalted	-44	0 (1 Cup)
Whipped	-24	0 (1 Cup)

Margarine (1 Tbsp)

	IF	GL
Butter Blend	-17	0 (1 Tbsp)
Stick Reduced Fat	-10	0 (1 Tbsp)
Tub Reduced Fat	-5	0 (1 Tbsp)

Sesame Seed Butter

	IF	GL
Tahini 1/4 Cup	-20	0 (1 Tbsp)

Mayonnaise (1 Tbsp)

	IF	GL
Light	-13	11 (1 Cup)
Soybean & Safflower Oil	-60	0 (1 Cup)
Soybean Oil (Hellman's)	-37	0 (1 Cup)
Tofu	-11	2 (1 Cup)
Cholesterol Free	-33	1 (1 Cup)

Honey

	IF	GL
1 Tbsp	-78	169 (1 Cup)

Maple Syrup

	IF	GL
1 Tbsp	-58	126 (1 Cup)

	IF	GL
Molasses		
1 Tbsp	-69	155 (1 Cup)
Peanut Butter (2 Tbsp)		
Reduced Fat	-21	4 (1 Oz)
Cream Cheese (1 Oz)		
Regular	-48	2 (1 Oz)
Fat Free	-7	1 (1 Oz)
Reduced Fat	-30	11 (1 Cup)

DRESSINGS
IF (2 Tbsp) GL (1 Cup)

	IF	GL
Bacon Tomato	-22	0
Blue Cheese	-39	0
Fat Free	-24	29
Light	-13	16
Buttermilk Light	-20	1
Caesar	-42	0
Fat Free	-35	
Light	-16	16
Coleslaw	-38	22
Light	-36	
French	-21	2
Fat Free	-28	35
Light	-17	30

	IF	GL
Green Goddess	-27	0
Honey Mustard	-36	4
Honey Fat Free	-41	
Honey Light	-14	
Italian	-16	4
Fat Free	-6	8
Light	-8	2
Oil & vinegar	-36	
Balsamic Vinegar		
(1 Tbsp)	-7	
Peppercorn	-52	
Poppyseed Creamy	-46	
Ranch	-41	0
Light	-19	1
Russian	-41	32
Light	-27	30
Sesame	-36	0
Thousand Island	-26	9
Fat Free	-25	34
Light	-3	1 (2 Tbsp)

SEASONINGS/ROOTS/SWEETENERS

	IF	GL
Persimmon		
Fresh 1/2 Cup (Native)	-19	4 (1 Fruit)
Fresh ½ Cup (Japanese)		8 (1 Fruit)
Dried 1/4 Cup	-51	11 (1 Fruit)
Soy Sauce (1 Tbsp)		
Shoyu	-3	11 (1 Cup)
Shoyu Low Sodium	-2	12 (1 Cup)
Tamari	-4	1 (1 Tbsp)
Soy Pasta		
Dried 1 Oz	-100	
Sugar		
Brown	-77	150 (1 Cup)
Granulated	-63	2 (1 Packet)
Powder	-42	84 (1 Cup)
Sucralose (Splenda)		
1 Packet	-4	1
Aspartame (Equal)		
1 Packet	-5	0
Tomato Paste/Sauce		
Paste 2 Tbsp	-4	9 (1 Cup)
Puree 1/2 Cup	-12	8 (1 Cup)
Sauce 1/2 Cup	-6	6 (1 Cup)
Sauce w/ Cheese 1/2 Cup	-39	
w/ Mushrooms 1/2 Cup	-3	8 (1 Cup)

Tofu (1/2 Cup)	IF	GL
Soft	-17	2 (1 Slice)
Firm	-22	2 (1 Slice)
Silken Light Firm	-24	1 (1 Slice)
Cinnamon		
Ground 1/2 Tsp	-1	1 (1 Tbsp)

DESSERTS
IF (1 Oz) GL (1 Piece)

Danish (1 Oz)		
Cheese	-30	14
Cinnamon	-33	35
Fruit	-46	37
Lemon	-52	19
Nut	-34	16
Pie Crust (1 Oz)		
Chocolate Cookie	-55	72
Frozen	-46	58
Graham Cracker	-49	86
Refrigerated	-92	98
Vanilla Wafer	-54	11
Cream		
Half & Half (1 Tbsp)	-8	-8
Fat Free	-5	1 (1 Oz)
Heavy	-18	0 (1 Cup)
Heavy Whipped 2 Tbsp	-18	0 (1 Cup)

	IF	GL
Light 1 Tbsp	-16	1 (1 Cup)
Table	-12	6
Liquid Light	-3	6
Powdered	-11	29
Powdered Light	-6	48 (1 Cup)
Croissant (1 Oz)		
Apple	-46	11 (1 Med.)
Cheese	-61	11 (Small)
Plain (Butter)	-63	7
Pie (1 Oz)		
Apple	-36	21
Banana Cream	-39	208
Blueberry	-35	22
Boston Cream	-46	21
Cherry	-37	26
Chocolate Cream	-61	15
Chocolate Mousse/ Mix	-38	14
Coconut Cream	-41	12
Coconut Custard	-33	16
Dutch Apple	-44	34
Egg Custard	-24	10
Fried Cherry	-40	27 (1 Pie)
Fried Fruit	-39	27 (1 Pie)
Fried Lemon	-40	27 (1 Pie)
Lemon Meringue	-63	29
Mince	-54	44

	IF	GL
Peach	-33	19
Pecan	-63	49
Pumpkin	-26	181
Vanilla Cream	-40	22

DESSERTS – COOKIES
IF (1 Oz) GL (1 Cookie)

	IF	GL
Chocolate Chip	-102	4
Reduced Fat	-99	5
Slice & Bake	-88	
Sandwich	-86	6
Extra Filling	-59	5
Wafer	-100	50 (1 Cup)
Devil's Food Fat Free	-105	11
Coconut Macaroon	-126	12
Brownie	-68	21
Animal Crackers	-92	36 (1 Box)
Fig Bars	-86	18
Fortune Cookie	-122	5
Frosted Lemon	-87	
Fruit & Honey	-96	
Ginger Snap	-99	4
Graham Cracker	-105	43 (1 Cup)
Chocolate Coated	-135	6

	IF	GL
Hermit	-97	12
Lady Finger	-106	5
Marshmallow Chocolate Coated	-75	11
Molasses	-93	16
Oatmeal W/Raisins	-74	7
Oatmeal Slice & Bake	-73	5
Peanut Butter	-64	5
Sandwich	-74	6
Slice & Bake	-72	5
Pecan Shortbread	-51	5
Raisin	-82	
Shortbread	-71	3
Sugar	-81	7
Sugar Wafer w/		
Cream Filling	-112	4
Slice & Bake	-75	6
Vanilla Wafer	-82	3
Reduced Fat	-99	38 (1 Cup)
Sandwich W/ Cream Filling	-99	7
White Macadamia Nut		17

DESSERTS - ICE CREAM

	IF	GL
Ice Cream Bar (1 Bar)		
Chocolate Covered	-86	
Crunch Coating	-300	
Chocolate (1/2 Cup)	-83	8
Light	-78	9
Light Sugar Free	-90	9
Premium	-93	15
Soft Serve Chocolate	-99	11 (1/2 Cup)
Light	-86	
Vanilla	-79	8
Fat Free	-73	4
Light	-97	10
Light Sugar Free	-75	7
Premium	-158	12
Soft Serve	-99	11 (1/2 Cup)
Light	-73	9
Dairy Queen Cones		
Chocolate		20
Vanilla		19
Dipped Chocolate		22
Breyers (1/2 Cup) (GL Only)		
Chocolate 98% Fat Free		9
Vanilla 98% Fat Free		9
Light French Choc.		11
Light French Vanilla		9

	IF	GL
Light Mint Choc. Chip		10
Light Vanilla Choc. Straw.		9
Vanilla Fudge Twirl (No Sugar)		9
Choc. Caramel (No Sugar)		9
Butter Pecan (No Sugar)		7

DESSERTS – DOUGHNUTS
IF (1 Oz) GL (1 Doughnut)

	IF	GL
Chocolate Sugar Glazed	-56	19
Cruller Sugar or Glazed	-65	15
Plain	-36	13
Chocolate Frosted	-73	5
Sugar or Glazed	-52	20
Wheat Sugar or Glazed	-45	6
Cream Filled	-16	13
Jelly Filled	-34	18
Raised Glazed	-62	

DESSERTS – CHOCOLATE

	IF	GL
Chocolate Soda (8 Oz)	-33	1 (1 Oz Carbonated beverage)
Baking Unsweetened (1 Oz)	-36	0 (1 Cup)
Dark Chocolate (1 Oz)	-77	13 (1 Bar)
Extra Dark (1 Oz)	-64	
70-85% Cocoa		15 (1 Bar)
60-69% Cocoa		26 (1 Bar)
45-59% Cocoa		46 (1 Bar)
Milk (1 Oz)	-103	13 (1 Cup)
Semi-Sweet (1 Oz)	-81	47
Cocoa Powder Unsweetened (1 Tbsp)	-2	16 (3 Tsp)
Cocoa from Mix (8 Oz)	-45	1 (1 Oz)
Sugar Free From Mix (8 Oz)	-93	2 (1 Oz)
Chocolate Syrup		16 (2 Tbsp)

COCONUT
IF (Varies) GL (1 Cup)

	IF	GL
Milk Canned (1/2 Cup)	-239	5
Coconut Water (8 Oz)	-18	3
Coconut Dried (1/4 Cup)	-100	0 (1 Oz)
Dried-Sweetened (1/4 Cup)	-77	22
Dried-Toasted (1/4 Cup)	-104	6 (1 Oz)
Raw (1/4 Cup)	-56	1

GRANOLA
IF (1/2 Cup) GL (1/2 Cup)

	IF	GL
Homemade	-92	31
Kellogg's Low Fat w/o Raisins	-82	27
Low Fat w/Raisins	-96	31
Nature Valley Low Fat w/ Fruit	-166	29
Quaker 100% Natural Low Fat w/ Raisins	-90	29
Quaker Oats & Honey	-113	21
Sun Country w/Almonds	-113	23

Granola Bars (1 Bar)

Hard plain		9
Coconut/Chocolate		8
Hard Almond		9

	IF	GL
Oats, Fruits, Nuts		14
Peanut Butter, Milk Choc.		10
Fruit Filled Non-Fat		13

OILS
IF (1 Tbsp) GL (1 Cup)

	IF	GL
Cocoa Butter	-40	0
Coconut	-115	0
Corn	-50	0
Cotton Seed	-94	0
Palm	-28	0
Palm Kernel	-99	0
Peanut	-3	0
Poppy Seed	-78	0
Rice Bran	-12	0
Safflower High Linoleic	-91	0
Sesame	-21	0
Soybean	-38	0
Sunflower Linoleic	-77	0
Walnut	-25	0
Wheat Germ	-54	0
Grapeseed	-87	0

POOR FAST FOOD CHOICES

IF Ratings Only

Pizza Hut (1 Pc)

Cheese-Stuffed Crust	-157
Pepperoni-Thin Crust	-137
Sausage-Classic Crust	-169
Sausage-Deep Dish	-190
Sausage-Thin Crust	-148

Domino's (1 Pc)

Sausage-Classic Crust	-169
Sausage-Deep Dish	-190
Sausage-Thin Crust	-114

1 Serving of the Following:

Applebee's Chicken Tender Platter	-303
Crunchy Onion Rings	-724
Burger King's Onion Rings	-350
Cracker Barrel's Onion Rings	-551
Fried Chicken Tenderloin Platter	-235
Denny's Chicken Strips	-277
Onion Rings	-357
Spaghetti & Meat-balls	-292
TGI Friday's Chicken Fingers	302

Wendy's Crispy Chicken Sandwich		-216
Subway 6" Roast Beef on White Bread		-118

Fast Foods with Cheese

	GL	Calories	Fat Grams
Carl's Junior (1 Order)			
American Cheese	0	49	4
Salad Dressing Blue Cheese	0	320	35
Swiss Style Cheese	0	50	4
Potato, Bacon Cheese	35	640	29
Cheese Danish Dessert	27	400	23
Del Taco (1 Order)			
Egg, Cheese Burrito	18	450	24
Chili, Cheese Fries	23	670	46
Deluxe Chili, Cheese Fries	24	710	49
Hardee's (1 Order)			
1/3 Bacon, Cheese, Thick Burger	23	910	63
2/3 Bacon, Cheese, Thick Burger	24	1,300	96

	GL	Calories	Fat Grams
Hot Ham 'n Cheese Sandwich	14	287	13
Big Hot Ham 'n Cheese Sandwich	20	435	20
Chili, Cheese Fries	31	700	39

Chick-Fil-A (1 Order)

	GL	Calories	Fat Grams
Bacon, Egg, Cheese Biscuit	20	470	26
Sausage, Egg, Cheese Biscuit	23	630	40
Egg, Cheese Biscuit	19	400	21
Chicken, Cheese Biscuit	23	470	23
Chicken, Egg, Cheese Bagel	24	500	20
Blue Cheese Dressing (1 Tbsp)	0	150	16

Hot Pockets (1 Pkg)

	GL	Calories	Fat Grams
Ham 'n Cheese	42	681	28

Little Caesar's Pizza (1 Slice)

	GL	Calories	Fat Grams
14" Cheese, Deep Dish	16	268	10
14" Cheese, Thin Crust	5	148	8
14" Cheese, Regular Crust	14	236	8

	GL	Calories	Fat Grams
McDonald's (1 Order)			
Bacon, Egg, Cheese Biscuit	15	432	27
Double Quarter Pounder w/Cheese	18	760	48
Quarter Pounder w/ Cheese	19	513	28
Ham, Egg, Cheese Bagel	30	550	23
Cheese Danish Dessert	25	400	21
Papa John's Pizza (1 Slice)			
14" Cheese Original Crust	20	304	11
14" Cheese Thin Crust	11	257	14
Cheese Dipping Sauce	1	70	6
Blue Cheese Dipping Sauce	0	170	18
Pizza Hut (1 Slice)			
14" Cheese Regular Crust	17	271	11
14" Thin Crust	11	225	10
Blue Cheese Dressing	0	140	14

	GL	Calories	Fat Grams
Subway Sandwich (6") & Soup (1 Order)			
Steak & Cheese	22	390	14
Salad Steak & Cheese	8	180	8
Cheese & Egg	16	320	15
Soup: Potato, Cheese Chowder	11	210	10
Broccoli & Cheese	4	180	12
Taco Bell (1 Order)			
Chili, Cheese Burrito	19	390	18
Chalupa Nacho Cheese Steak	12	340	21
Chalupa Nacho Cheese Chicken	12	340	20
Nacho Cheese Sauce	2	110	10
Cheese Quesadilla	18	490	29
Wendy's (1 Order)			
Jr. Hamburger w/Cheese	16	330	15
Hot Stuffed Baked Potato Bacon w/Cheese	37	580	22
Egg, Sausage, Cheese Biscuit	10	460	34
Blue Cheese Dressing			
2 Tbsp	0	70	6

Summary

Food measurements for counting calories uses weight in grams. The following three nutrients are most important:

1 Gram of a Carbohydrate = 4 calories

1 Gram of a Protein = 4 calories

1 Gram of a Fat or Alcohol = 9 calories

Basically, a carbohydrate is everything non-animal or fish. In terms of calories, the non-starchy vegetables contain but 20-25 calories per ½ cup yet require about 15-20 calories for digestion. Try to gain weight here. Whether pro-inflammatory or anti-inflammatory, these figures apply. Pro-inflammatory non-starchy vegetables also have an insignificant negative **IF** ratings. Starchy vegetables, whether pro- inflammatory or anti-inflammatory, carry approximately 70 calories, but the negative IF rating for pro-inflammatory starchy vegetables is quite significant.

So what's the answer? Eat non-starchy vegetables primarily from the anti-inflammatory list and trickle in some from the pro- inflammatory side. Starch is an important nutrient, so limit it to the anti-inflammatory side. That takes care of your vegetables. How hard can that be? No worry about counting calories, figuring portion sizes, and juggling the all-important inflammation issue.

For cooking oils, stay on the anti-inflammatory side; there are plenty! Those on the pro-inflammatory side are a huge risk for the most part.

Meats are mostly favorable in terms of **IF** rating, but stay away from animal organs. Beef is a good choice, but surprisingly, chicken needs to be accompanied by strictly anti-inflammatory vegetables, especially peppers and chili peppers. Chili peppers are off the chart anti-inflammatory.

The difficult task comes from sifting through mainstream health articles and promotions.

I just received an article touting coconut oil for cooking. It has a long shelf-life and can resist creating high heat carcinogens; cancer promoters. It's even been shown to improve cognitive qualities of those with Alzheimer's disease. Believe me, it tastes good. However, its **IF** rating is -115; moderately high at one tablespoon. That single tablespoon might not be enough for cooking. Three tablespoons and your **IF** rating now equals -345. Toss in some beef liver and you have another -143; total now is -478. That's a big hole to climb out from. You probably will not be able to avoid finishing the meal on the pro-inflammation side.

The same beef liver at -143 fried in canola oil at +80, gives you a reasonable start of -63. Toss some cooked carrots on your plate at +130 and your result is a friendly +73. If you don't like cooked carrots, place a baked sweet potato on your plate at +189, and your result is a whopping +146.

Honey has been praised weekly in my email inbox for its wonderful qualities. One tablespoon of God's food is a -78. It has been pushed ferociously to replace all sweeteners. Besides the rather dreadful negative **IF** rating, its glycemic load (GL) indicator is off the chart at 169; anything over 20 is awful. Use judiciously. Sweeten your cereal with strawberries. I love honey, but I am "in love" with a healthy body, seeing how like everyone else, I get only one.

Too many "health practitioners" are only concerned with the outer body composition. If you are "roped in" to mainstream hysteria, you'll "hollow-out" yourself. But, you'll leave an attractive corpse for the viewing. Gimmicks do not work anywhere in life.

Anytime you read about or are told of a food's healthy qualities, check this book for its **IF** rating. A poor **IF** rating will trump the food's nutritious value. It's then time to find an alternative food with a positive **IF** rating.

An occasional delicious processed (boxed, packaged, etc.) food will make eating and living somewhat worthwhile. But if you live out of the box or package, there is no hope for you. At some point, that insistence on ignoring the inevitable reality will leave you with depressing deathbed regrets. All you can really hope for is listening resides on your "hard drive."

> Every man has a right to his opinion, but no man has a right to be wrong with his facts.
>
> -Bernard W. Baruch

www.ingramcontent.com/pod-product-compliance
Lightning Source LLC
LaVergne TN
LVHW012247070526
838201LV00090B/144